# Mini Instant Pot Cookbook

Over 200 Proven, Delicious & Easy Recipes for Mini Instant Pot 3 Quart Models

# Table of Contents

# Introduction

The Instant Pot Mini is a great appliance. Although small, it has the same awesome features of the larger models of its family.

### *Everything You Need To Know About Mini Instant Pot*

Although as awesome as any larger cooker, how does the mini differ from them?

### Lower Cooking Pressure

While most of the pressure cooker models operate at 80kPa (11.6 psi), the minis work at 70kPa (10.1 psi) for HIGH pressure. For its LOW pressure mode, it cooks at 50kPa (7.2 psi), which means lower cooking temperature.

### Lesser Time to Achieve Pressure

The mini's smaller size means that the appliance achieves pressure is significantly shorter time than larger models. Although the differences are not huge, it will affect the cooking process of tougher foods that take a longer time to cook, such as cheaper meats, dense veggies, and whole grains. Tests reveal that while larger cookers take an average of 13 minutes, the minis reaches the right pressure in 9 minutes.

The difference significantly affects cooking time since the dish in the pot is cooking while your pot is both building and losing steam pressure. Generally, the 4-minute difference in reaching pressure means 2 minutes less of cooking time.

Together with the reduced working temperature due to the lower pressure, you will need to add between 2 to 15 minutes to the total cooking time when adapting recipes for larger cookers to the mini.

### Top 10 Secrets to Utilize Mini Instant Pot to Its Fullest Potential

In a world where most pressure cooker recipes are cooked for larger appliances, mostly 6-quarts, here are valuable tips on how you can use your 3-quart mini pot to its fullest potential in the kitchen.

It is not as easy as cutting down the ingredients for the recipe. There are various hidden modifications and variances can hugely affect how dishes are cooked for the mini models. These are the variables you need to keep in mind.

### Use Less Cooking Liquid

While larger models require 1 1/2 cups liquid, cooking tests reveal that you can use as little as 1 1/4 cups for the mini. Take note that part of the cooking juices will come from the ingredients themselves so you can eventually use less than that and the pot can still achieve pressure, assuming that the ingredients will release more.

## Use Less Ingredients

Always remember to keep in mind the maximum-fill guidelines. You should never fill it more than half with ingredients that create foam or expands, such as beans, grains, and rice. Likewise, never fill it 2/3-full for most foods.

In this note, for the mini, never fill the pot with more than 7 cups veggies & 1 cup liquid, 3 1/2 pound of meat & 1 cup liquid, 2 cups dry rice & 3 cups water, or 2 cups beans & 4 cups water. Take note, the "cup" I refer to here is 8-ounce or 250 ml U.S. measurement.

## Cooking Time Remains the Same

You do not need to adjust the cooking time for most recipes since the duration is generally based on the density and size of the ingredients. No matter how much you are using, if density and size are the same, use the same cooking time.

However, if cooking very dense ingredients, you have to adjust cooking time to compensate for the lower pressure of the mini.

## Split All of the Ingredients

Obviously, the smaller size means that it can contain a lesser amount of ingredients. Always check if they will not exceed the maximum limit. You may need to reduce the ingredients to half or to 1/3 their original amount.

## Adjust the Cooking Liquid

Calculate if you need to alter the amount of cooking liquid as well. Use the right ratio needed for cooking grains and beans. If you reduced the solids by 1/2 or 1/3, you generally have to do the same for the liquid. However, do not go lower than the required amount to achieve pressure, which is 1 1/4 cups in minis.

## Use the Maximum Liquid for Soups

If you are cooking dishes that are supposed to be liquidy or soups, you can add enough cooking liquid to almost cover the food, just do not exceed the 2/3 maximum limit.

## Use the Minimum Liquid for Stews

If you are cooking dishes that are supposed to be braised or stews, then you can use the minimum cooking juices required since the ingredients will release moisture as well.

## Use the Minimum Amount for Pot-in-Pot Cooking or Steamed Recipes

Cooking liquid for steamed dishes or PIP recipes will generally require only the minimum required to achieve proper pressure.

## A Sling Foil is Handy for PIP Cooking

Pot-in-Pot cooking is a method where you place all the ingredients in a heatproof container that will fit your pot and place it on a trivet set in the IP with cooking liquid for pressure cooking.

Using a foil sling will allow you to lower the container and take it out safely. Just fold the sling unobtrusively in the pot.

### Sauté the Spices and Brown the Meat

Although doing these steps is optional and some recipes do not mention them, they will greatly enhance the flavor and texture of your recipes. So if you have time, do not just dump and cook the ingredients for your dishes.

### Top 5 Mistakes to Avoid

### No-Liquid-Added Recipes

There are many recipes going around that require no cooking liquid for pressure cooking. They claim that these dishes will not overheat the pot before the ingredients release moisture to allow the cooker to achieve proper pressure.

Some of these recipes may work, and some may not. The results are often unreliable and you may end up with undercooked, partially burnt food. Plus they may damage your appliance, which is not designed for dry cooking under pressure.

### Leaving Dishes on KEEP WARM

Although your pot will automatically switch to the engage "KEEP WARM" when the cooking time is complete to keep your dishes warm until you are ready to serve them, leaving them longer than 4 hours will make them lose their texture and flavor.

### Using Quick Pressure Release for Foamy, Thick, and Saucy Foods

Always allow the pressure to drop down naturally when you are cooking grains and beans, spaghetti, noodles, oatmeal, cereals, etc. to prevent hot liquid from sputtering from the nozzle and clogging it.

If you need to release the pressure quickly, then cover the nozzle with a clean towel to avoid any accidents and burns resulting from very hot steam.

### Quickly Releasing the Pressure Using Bare Hands

Always open the pressure release nozzle while wearing oven mitts. You can also turn it using tongs or a long-handled spoon. You can likewise cover it with a clean towel to avoid any accidents and burns resulting from very hot steam. Remember to set the nozzle away from people or any object that high heat can damage.

### Using the Same Sealing Ring

You will want to use a different sealing ring for your sweet food and savory dishes. If you use the same ring after making a chicken dinner for cooking an applesauce, you will end up with a dessert that has chicken flavor in it. So buy two rings for your pot to prevent wasting food for recipes you will end up throwing away.

# BREAKFAST

## Blueberry-Almond Casserole French Toast

Servings|**4**　Prep. Time|**5 minutes**　Cook Time|**25 minutes**
**Nut. Content (per serving):** Cal|**202**　Fat|**7.68g**　Protein|**8.49g**　Carbs|**25.2g**

1 cup blueberries (fresh) or 1/2 cup froze, thawed
1 cup milk (whole)
1/2 teaspoon almond extract
1/2 teaspoon cinnamon
1/4 cup sugar (brown)
2 eggs
4 French bread slices (thick), slice into 2-inch chunks

Cooking spray:
Almonds, slivered, to serve
Maple syrup to serve if desired
More Blueberries to serve
Powdered sugar to serve

Materials:
1-liter (1-quart) casserole dish (round baking), 5 1/2-inch diameter

1. Whisk the cinnamon, almond extract, sugar, eggs, and milk in a bowl (large) till mixed. Fold in the bread pieces and the blueberries till well coated. Grease the baking dish with some cooking spray. Pour the mixture in the dish.
2. Put the IP trivet in the inner pot and pour 3/4 cup water. Lower the dish on the trivet. Lock the lid and close the pressure valve. Set to HIGH PRESSURE for 25 minutes. QPR when the timer beeps; unlock the lid and open. Serve.

## Cream & Strawberry Rolled Oats

Servings|**1**　Prep. Time|**1 minute** Cook Time|**26 minutes**
**Nut. Content (per serving):** Cal|**207.8**　Fat|**7.3g**　Protein|**8.6g**　Carbs|**28.3g**

1/2 teaspoon (2 grams) white sugar
1/3 cup (35 grams) oats (rolled)
2 tablespoons (4 grams) strawberries (freeze-dried) or preferred frozen or dried fruit

2/3 cup (150 grams) milk (whole)
Pinch salt

1. Put the IP trivet in the inner pot and pour 2 cups water. In a heatproof mug or small bowl, add the salt, strawberries, and oats. Lock the lid and close the pressure valve. Set to HIGH PRESSURE for 10 minutes. Cancel the KEEP WARM mode and unplug when the timer beeps. NPR for 10 to 15 minutes or till the indicator is down and QPR; unlock the lid and open. Remove the mug or bowl from the pot carefully; mix the contents vigorously.  Sprinkle with sugar; serve.

# Breakfast Hash

Servings|**2 to 3**    Prep. Time|**10 minutes**    Cook Time|**30 minutes**
**Nut. Content (per 3 servings):** Cal|**262**    Fat|**13g**    Protein|**16.2g**    Carbs|**20.4g**

1 1/2 tablespoon butter
1 cup broth (chicken)
1 medium cloves garlic, peeled & minced (1 teaspoon)
1/2 medium bell pepper (green) stemmed, cored, & chopped (1/2 cup)
1/2 medium bell pepper (red) stemmed, cored, & chopped (1/2 cup)
1/2 onion (medium yellow), chopped (1/2 cup)

1/2 pound ham (smoked deli), do not use thinly shaved; remove any coating, meat diced
1/2 pound potatoes (yellow), diced (unpeeled)
1/2 teaspoon sage (dried)
1/2 teaspoon thyme (dried)
1/4 teaspoon celery seeds, optional
1/8 teaspoon black pepper (ground)
1/8 teaspoon salt (fine table)

1. Set the IP to SAUTE for 5 minutes. Add the butter; let melt. Add the bell peppers and onion; sauté for 4 minutes or till soft, stirring occasionally. Add the diced ham, salt, pepper, celery seeds, thyme, sage, and garlic; sauté for 1 minute or till fragrant, stirring often. Press CANCEL.
2. Stir in the diced potatoes and the broth; scrape any brown bits of the pot. Lock the lid and close the pressure valve. Set to HIGH PRESSURE for 12 minutes. QPR when the timer beeps; unlock the lid and open. Stir to mix well.
3. Set the IP to SAUTÉ for 10 minutes; let the mixture come to a simmer while stirring often. Continue stirring for 3 to 4 minutes or till the liquid cooks off and the underside of the hash starts to brown. Press CANCEL. Remove the inner pot from the housing. Serve.

# Perfectly Hard-Boiled Eggs

Servings|**6**    Prep. Time|**10 minutes**    Cook Time|**5 minutes**
**Nut. Content (per serving):** Cal|**62**    Fat|**4g**    Protein|**5g**    Carbs|**0g**

6 eggs (large)                                        1 cup water

1. Turn ON the IP. Put the IP steamer basket in the inner pot and pour 1 cup water. Put the eggs in the basket. Lock the lid and close the pressure valve. Set to HIGH PRESSURE for 5 minutes. NPR for 5 minutes when the timer beeps and QPR; unlock the lid and open. Transfer the eggs to a container with tap cold water; let sit and soak for 5 minutes. Remove from the water. Serve as is or use in salads, sandwiches, or any dish.

## Banana Bread Bundt

Servings|**8**    Prep. Time|**10 minutes**    Cook Time|**25 minutes**
**Nut. Content (per serving):** Cal|**274**    Fat|**10.6g**    Protein|**7g**    Carbs|**39.2g**

1 1/2 cups flour (all-purpose)
1 1/2 cups water
1 1/2 teaspoon baking soda
1 teaspoon vanilla extract
1/2 cup sugar (granulated white)
1/2 cup walnuts, almonds, pecans, or hazelnuts (skinned)

1/2 cup yogurt (plain), fat-free, regular, or low-fat
1/4 teaspoon salt (table)
2 eggs (large)
2 medium bananas (very ripe), peeled
2 tablespoons lemon juice (fresh)
3 tablespoon butter, bring to temperature
Baking spray (flour-&-fat)

1. Put the IP trivet in the inner pot and pour the water. Very generously grease the Bundt pan (7-inch), with baking spray, ensuring the fat gets in every nook and cranny.
2. Put the bananas, butter, eggs, and sugar in the food processor; cover and puree till smooth, scraping the sides as needed. Add the vanilla, lemon juice, and yogurt; cover and puree till smooth, scraping the sides as needed. Add the salt, baking soda, and flour; pulse till the batter is uniformly mixed. Add the nuts; pulse a bit to chop and mix them in.
3. Transfer the batter to the prepared pan. Smooth the top and even. If you want them perfect, then leave a 1/2-inch clear space from the top of the pan; discard the excess batter. Cover the pan with paper towel, making sure it does not touch the batter.
4. Lock the lid and close the pressure valve. Set to HIGH PRESSURE for 25 minutes. Cancel the KEEP WARM mode and unplug when the timer beeps. NPR for 10 to 15 minutes or till the indicator is down and QPR; unlock the lid and open.
5. Remove the paper towel. Lift the pan out from the pan to a cooling wire rack; let cool for 5 minutes. Invert it onto a plate; gently shake to dislodge. Return the cake on the cooling rack; let cool for at least 20 minutes before cutting into wedges.
NOTES: You can transfer the batter into a bowl after processing; fold in 1/2 cup chocolate chips (semi-sweet), dried cranberries, or raisins, before transferring in the pan.

# Loaded Cornbread Bundt

Servings|**8**    Prep. Time|**15 minutes**    Cook Time|**20 minutes**
**Nut. Content (per serving):** Cal|**219**    Fat|**9.3g**    Protein|**7.4g**    Carbs|**28.1g**

1 1/2 cups water
1 cup corn kernels (frozen), thawed
1 cup cornmeal (yellow)
1/2 teaspoon salt (table)
1/4 cup chopped green chilies (canned), mild or hot, (about 1/2 of a 4 1/2-ounce can)
2 eggs (large) bring to temperature
2 ounces mozzarella (semi-firm), shredded (around 1/2 cup)

2 teaspoons baking powder
2 teaspoons sugar (granulated white), use 1 tablespoon to emphasize the other flavors
3/4 cup buttermilk (regular)
3/4 cup flour (all-purpose)
4 tablespoons butter, melted & cooled to room temperature, with extra for greasing the pan

1. Whisk the salt, sugar, baking powder, flour, and cornmeal in a bowl (medium) till well mixed. Put the IP trivet in the inner pot and pour the water. Generously grease a 7-inch Bundt pan with the butter.
2. Whisk the buttermilk and eggs in a bowl (large) till creamy and smooth. Stir in the chilies, butter, mozzarella, and corn. Add the flour mixture; stir till the cornmeal and flour are moist and uniformly mixed in the batter. Transfer the batter in the prepared pan. If you want a perfect edge, leave a 1/2-inch clear space from the rim; discard excess batter.
3. Put the pan on the trivet. Lock the lid and close the pressure valve. Set to HIGH PRESSURE for 25 minutes. Cancel the KEEP WARM mode and unplug when the timer beeps. NPR for 10 to 15 minutes or till the indicator is down and QPR; unlock the lid and open.
4. Transfer the pan to a cooling wire rack. Let cool for 5 to 10 minutes. To unmold, place a slicing board on top of the pan. Flip the board and the pan at the same time upside-down. Jiggle the pan to loosen the cake; remove the pan. Invert the cake sit right side up. Let cool for 10 minutes more before slicing into wedges.

# Vegetable Quinoa Pilaf

Servings | **3**   Prep. Time | **10 minutes**   Cook Time | **15 minutes**
**Nut. Content (per serving):** Cal | **196**   Fat | **6g**   Protein | **6g**   Carbs | **28g**

1 gold potato (medium), chunked into 1/4-inch cubes (around 3/4 cup)
1 onion (small), sliced thin (around 3/4 cup)
1 tablespoon olive oil
1 teaspoon coriander powder
1 teaspoon ketchup, optional, but recommended
1 teaspoon mustard seeds
1/2 cup peas (frozen)
1/2 cup quinoa, rinsed in a sieve (mesh)
1/2 cup water
1/2 teaspoon chili powder (red)

2 green chilies, optional
2 teaspoons ginger (fresh), chopped finely or grated; or 1/2 teaspoon ginger powder)
3/4 teaspoon salt
3/4 teaspoon turmeric powder
6 leaves curry or 1 leaf kaffir lime

Garnish:
1 teaspoon (1/2 piece) lime juice
1/4 teaspoon sugar
2 tablespoons cilantro, chopped

1. Set the IP to SAUTE. Once HOT, add the oil and mustard seeds. Once spluttering, add the potatoes, curry leaves, green chili, onions, and ginger; sauté for 1 minute. Add the peas, cashews, quinoa, water, ketchup, and all the dry spices; stir to mix well.
2. Lock the lid and close the pressure valve. Set to HIGH PRESSURE for 1 minute or for 2 minutes for a softer quinoa. NPR for 5 minutes when the timer beeps and QPR; unlock the lid and open. Fluff the quinoa using a fork. Add the sugar, cilantro, and lime juice; stir using a fork. Serve warm.

## Cinnamon Raisin Casserole French Toast

Servings|**8**    Prep. Time|**10 minutes**    Cook Time|**15 minutes**
**Nut. Content (per serving):** Cal|**157**    Fat|**4g**    Protein|**5g**    Carbs|**24g**

1 tablespoon maple syrup
1/2 cup milk (preferably 2% fat)
2 eggs (large)
4 slices bread (cinnamon raisin, store-bought)

Broiling (optional):
2 teaspoon butter, chopped or thinly sliced
2 tablespoon sugar (brown)

1. Lightly grease a cake pan or ovenproof bowl with some oil or butter. Slice the bread into 1-inch cubes. Add to the bowl. Whisk the maple syrup, eggs, and milk till well mixed. Pour over the bread; press down lightly so the bread absorbs the milk mixture. Let sit for 5 minutes. Cover the container with foil.
2. Put the IP trivet in the inner pot and pour 1 to 2 cups water. Put the container on the trivet. Lock the lid and close the pressure valve. Set to HIGH PRESSURE for 15 minutes. QPR when the timer beeps; unlock the lid and open.
3. Preheat the oven to 375F. Bake for 35 to 40 minutes or till fully cooked. Carefully remove from the oven.
4. Optional topping (highly recommended): Slice the butter into thin pieces. Put all over the toast. Evenly sprinkle the sugar on the top. Broil for 1 to 2 minutes or till the butter melts and the sugar is caramelized. Let cool for 5 minutes. Pour maple syrup over the toast. Serve.

## Maple Syrup Oats

Servings|**1**    Prep. Time|**1 minute** Cook Time|**20 minutes**
**Nut. Content (per serving):** Cal|**240**    Fat|**8.3g**    Protein|**6.1g**    Carbs|**40.5g**

3/4 cup (170 grams) water
1/4 cup (40 grams) oats (steel-cut, quick-cooking)

1/2 tablespoon butter
1 tablespoon maple syrup (100%)
Pinch salt

1. Put the IP trivet in the inner pot and pour 2 cups water. In a heatproof mug or small bowl, add the butter, salt, water, and oats. Put the bowl on the trivet. Lock the lid and close the pressure valve. Set to HIGH PRESSURE for 3 minutes.
2. Cancel the KEEP WARM mode and unplug when the timer beeps. NPR for 10 to 15 minutes or till the indicator is down and QPR; unlock the lid and open.
3. Remove the mug or bowl from the pot carefully; mix the contents vigorously. Drizzle with maple syrup; serve.

# Soy Milk

Servings | **4**    Prep. Time | **10 minutes**    Cook Time | **25 minutes**
**Nut. Content (per 8 oz.):** Cal | **113.4**    Fat | **5g**    Protein | **9.1g**    Carbs | **8g**

1 vanilla bean pod, optional
1/2 cup (100 grams) soybeans (organic yellow)
1/2 teaspoon sugar (raw), optional

5 cups (1250 milliliters) water, plus extra for blending
Pinch salt (sea), optional

1. Soak the soybeans in plenty of water for 24 to 36 hours. Strain, rinse well and change the water around halfway through soaking time. Strain and rinse again before using.
2. Transfer the soybeans in a chopper (small), such as the one that comes with your immersion blender. Add 1/2 cup of water. Puree using the highest power for 90 seconds.
3. Transfer the pureed raw soybeans in the IP using a heatproof spatula; Add 5 cups water; mix to stir well, make sure the total content does not exceed the pot's 1/2 full mark. Set to SAUTE and let come to a boil, occasionally stirring using the spatula. The soy is boiling when the foam volume increases quickly. With a skimmer, remove the foam from the top and discard, wiping down the sides of the pot using the spatula, and give the mixture one final stir.
4. Lock the lid and close the pressure valve. Set to HIGH PRESSURE for 9 minutes. Cancel the KEEP WARM mode and unplug when the timer beeps. NPR for 10 to 15 minutes or till the indicator is down and QPR; unlock the lid and open.
5. While the pot is depressurizing, put the sugar, salt, and vanilla bean in a wide mouth bowl or pitcher; set a strainer (fine mesh) on top. Carefully pour the hot soybean through the strainer; push down on the pulp using the spatula to wring the rest of the milk.
6. Stir the contents of the bowl or pitcher well. Let it cool. Remove and rinse the vanilla bean to use for another batch. Save the soybean pulp to make other dishes, such as homemade bread. Cover the bowl/pitcher tightly. Keep the soymilk refrigerated for 3 to 4 days. Shake well before each use.
NOTES: For more vanilla flavor, slice the pod crosswise in half and then lengthwise. Only use half of the pod to give the milk a stronger vanilla taste.

# Mini Cornbread Squares

Servings | **2 (4 muffins)**     Prep. Time | **10 minutes**     Cook Time | **12 minutes**
**Nut. Content (per serving):** Cal | **0**     Fat | **0g**     Protein | **0g**     Carbs | **0g**

1 cup water, for the IP

Wet ingredients:
1 1/4 tablespoons butter, melted
1 egg
1/3 cup milk

Dry ingredients:
1 1/4 teaspoons baking powder
1 tablespoon PLUS 1 teaspoon sugar
1/3 cup cornmeal
1/3 cup flour (all-purpose)
1/4 teaspoon salt

1. Grease a small, oven-safe or food silicon ice cube tray with 4 pieces 2-inch openings or a similar container with a cooking spray; set aside. Sift the dry ingredients into a mixing bowl (small).

2. Add the egg to a cup; beat it using a fork. Add the butter and milk; whisk to mix well. Add the wet ingredients to the dry ingredients; gently mix till the dry ingredients are just moistened, but not over-mixed – few dry spots are fine. Divide the batter between the openings equally. Cover with foil.

3. Put the IP trivet in the inner pot and pour 1 cup water. Put the container on the trivet. Lock the lid and close the pressure valve. Set to MANUAL PRESSURE HIGH for 13 minutes. NPR for 15 minutes when the timer beeps and QPR; unlock the lid and open.

4. Remove the container from the pot; let rest for 5 minutes. Remove the foil, flip the tray upside down over a plate, and gently press on the bottom to unmold the muffins. Slather with maple syrup, honey, butter, or with your preferred cornbread. This pair well with chili, black beans, or serve as a snack.

# POULTRY

## Cajun Chicken Salad

Servings|**4**    Prep. Time|**10 minutes**    Cook Time|**30 minutes**
**Nut. Content (per serving):** Cal|**289**    Fat|**18g**    Protein|**25g**    Carbs|**4g**

1 pound chicken (thighs or breast), boneless & skinless

Salad dressing (makes 2 servings):
1 tablespoon vinegar (apple cider)
1 teaspoon mustard (honey Dijon)
1/4 teaspoon black pepper (fresh ground), adjust to preference
1/4 teaspoon salt (adjust to preference)
3 tablespoon olive oil (extra-virgin)

Wet rub:
1/2 lime, juiced
1 teaspoon salt
1 tablespoon olive oil (extra light)
1 tablespoon Cajun seasoning

Salad (makes 1 portion):
1 tablespoon sliced almonds, toasted
1 to 2 radish (small), sliced thin, optional
2 cups preferred lettuce or cabbage slaw salad mix
4 strawberries, sliced thin

1. Wet rub: In a resealable bag (large) or mixing bowl, mix the Cajun seasoning, lime juice, salt, or olive oil. Add the chicken in the bag, seal, and shake to coat well with the rub. Marinate in the fridge for at least 20 minutes to 4 hours.
2. Put the IP trivet in the inner pot and pour 1 cup water. Put the chicken on the trivet. Lock the lid and close the pressure valve. Set to MANUAL HIGH PRESSURE for 8 minutes for breast or for 6 minutes for thighs. NPR for 10 minutes when the timer beeps and QPR; unlock the lid and open. Transfer to a slicing board; let rest for 10 minutes before slicing.
3. Optional step: Heat a skillet. Sear both sides of the chicken for 1 minute to add the grilled flavor to the chicken. Alternatively, you can broil them.
4. Assembly: Mix all of the salad ingredients in a bowl (large). Mix all the dressing ingredients in a small bowl or Mason jar till well combined. Pour the dressing over the salad. Slice the chicken; top on the salad. Serve.

## Herb Citrus Chicken

Servings|4   Prep. Time|6 minutes   Cook Time|30 minutes
**Nut. Content (per serving):** Cal|570   Fat|21.2g   Protein|47.2g   Carbs|4.4g

1 teaspoon rosemary (fresh), chopped
1/2 cups tangerine juice
1/4 cups lemon juice
1/4 cups wine (white)
1/4 teaspoons thyme (dried)

1/8 teaspoons black pepper
1/8 teaspoons salt
2 1/2 pounds (bone-in) chicken thighs
2 teaspoons cloves garlic, minced

1. Put the chicken in the IP. Mix the pepper, salt, thyme, rosemary, garlic, wine, tangerine juice, and lemon juice in a bowl. Pour the sauce over the chicken. Lock the lid and close the pressure valve. Set to HIGH PRESSURE for 30 minutes. NPR for 5 minutes when the timer beeps and QPR; unlock the lid and open. Serve.

## Tangy Hunter Chicken

Servings|4   Prep. Time|10 minutes   Cook Time|20 minutes
**Nut. Content (per serving):** Cal|748   Fat|029.3g   Protein|50g   Carbs|12.5g

1 tablespoon oil (vegetable)
1 teaspoon oregano (dried)
1 teaspoon rosemary (dried)
1 teaspoon thyme (dried)
1/2 onion (medium), sliced
1/2 teaspoon pepper
1/2 teaspoon salt
1/4 cup wine (red), optional, or broth
(chicken) or water

2 cloves garlic, peeled & minced
28 ounces (canned) diced tomatoes packed with juice
3 pounds chicken thighs or quarters (skin-on & bone-in)
8 ounces mushrooms, sliced

1. Set the IP to SAUTE. Once HOT, add the oil; heat till shimmering. Add the mushrooms, onion, and garlic; sauté for 5 minutes or till the mushrooms release their moisture. Add the wine; scrape the brown bits off the pot. With the skin under, put the chicken on top of the mushroom mixture. Press CANCEL.
2. Add the rosemary, tomatoes, 1/2 cup water, thyme, oregano, pepper, and salt; stir to mix. Lock the lid and close the pressure valve. Set to HIGH PRESSURE for 20 minutes. QPR when the timer beeps; unlock the lid and open.
3. Stir to mix the ingredients. Transfer the chicken to a serving plate with tongs. Pour the sauce over them. Serve with favorite polenta dish.

## Better Version Butter Chicken

Servings|**3**    Prep. Time|**5 minutes**    Cook Time|**12 minutes**
**Nut. Content (per serving):** Cal|**557**    Fat|**26.1g**    Protein|**34.3g**    Carbs|**9.3g**

1 1/2 pounds chicken breasts (bone-in & skinless), slice widthwise into halves
1 tablespoon curry powder (yellow)
1/2 tablespoon ginger (fresh), peeled & minced
1/2 yellow onion (small) chopped (1/4 cup)

1/4 cup broth (chicken) or wine (dry white)
1/4 cup cream (heavy)
1/8 teaspoon salt (table)
2 tablespoons (1/4 stick) butter, sliced into bits
3/4 cup crushed tomatoes (canned)

1. Set the IP to SAUTE for 5 minutes. Mix the onion, tomato, wine/broth, salt, ginger, curry powder, and butter in the pot; sauté for 2 minutes or till the butter melts, stirring occasionally. Press CANCEL. Add the chicken; mix to coat well with the sauce.
2. Lock the lid and close the pressure valve. Set to MEAT/STEW for 15 minutes. QPR when the timer beeps; unlock the lid and open. Transfer the chicken to individual serving bowls or serving platter.
3. Set the IP to SAUTÉ for 5 minutes. Let the sauce come to a simmer while stirring. Stir in the cream, cook while stirring briskly for 2 minutes till thick. Press CANCEL. Scoop the sauce over the chicken. Serve over sweet potatoes (baked, split open) or cauliflower rice.

## Chicken Breasts Perfectly-Seared

Servings|**2**    Prep. Time|**10 minutes**    Cook Time|**13 minutes**
**Nut. Content (per serving):** Cal|**599**    Fat|**27.8g**    Protein|**41g**    Carbs|**0g**

1 tablespoon mix of preferred dried herbs, Greek, French, Italian, Cajun, herbes de Provence, etc.
1 tablespoon preferred liquid or solid cooking fat
1/4 teaspoon salt (table) optional

2 chicken breasts (boneless & skinless), 10 to 12 ounces each
3/4 cups preferred cooking liquid, water, any kind of broth, dry sherry, dry vermouth, etc.

1. Set the IP to SAUTE for 15 minutes. Add the fat, let melt if solid, and warm. Season the chicken with the herbs and optional salt. Put the breasts in the pot; cook for 6 minutes or till well browned, flipping once. Transfer to a plate; set aside. Press CANCEL.
2. Put the IP trivet in the inner pot and pour the cooking liquid. Put the chicken on the trivet, overlapping the thin ends over the thick ends as needed. Lock the lid and close the pressure valve. Set to HIGH PRESSURE for 8 minutes. Cancel the KEEP WARM mode and unplug when the timer beeps. NPR for 10 to 15 minutes or till the indicator is down and QPR; unlock the lid but do not open and let sit for 3 minutes. Serve garnished with plenty of black pepper (ground).

# Fried Chicken

Servings|**3**    Prep. Time|**15 minutes**    Cook Time|**15 minutes**
**Nut. Content (per serving):** Cal|**543**    Fat|**21g**    Protein|**41.2g**    Carbs|**0.9g**

3 chicken thighs (skin-on & bone-in), 8 to 10 ounces each
3/4 cups water
Preferred frying oil

Seasoning:
1/2 teaspoon onion powder
1/4 teaspoon black pepper (ground)
1/4 teaspoon sage (dried)
1/4 teaspoon thyme (dried)
1/8 teaspoon garlic powder
3/4 teaspoon paprika (mild)
3/4 teaspoon salt (kosher)

1. Mix the spices in a plate (large) till well combined. Pat the chicken dry using paper towels. Roll the chicken in the spice mixture till thoroughly and evenly coated.
2. Put the IP trivet in the inner pot and pour the water. Stack the thighs on the trivet. Lock the lid and close the pressure valve. Set to HIGH PRESSURE for 15 minutes. QPR when the timer beeps; unlock the lid and open. Transfer the chicken paper towel-lined rimmed sheet pan (large). Set aside for at least 20 minutes to 1 hour to dry.
3. Place a skillet (12-inch) on medium flame/heat. Add enough oil to reach 1/2-inch deep. Let heat till shimmering. Add the chicken in the skillet; fry for 10 minutes or till crisp and golden. Turn and cook for 10 minutes till the other side is crisp, golden, and cooked through. Transfer to a cooling wire rack; season with salt if desired.

# Thanksgiving Pulled Turkey

Servings|**4**    Prep. Time|**10 minutes**    Cook Time|**25 minutes**
**Nut. Content (per serving):** Cal|**264**    Fat|**7.3g**    Protein|**42.5g**    Carbs|**4g**

1 1/4 pounds turkey tenderloins, boneless & skinless
1 tablespoon packed fresh sage leaves chopped finely
1 teaspoon thyme (fresh) leaves
1/2 cup broth (chicken)

1/2 sweet potato (small), peeled & shredded using the large holes of your box grater
1/2 teaspoon salt (table)
1/4 cup cranberry sauce (whole berry)

1. Mix the cranberry sauce, broth, salt, thyme, and sage in the IP. Stir in the potato. Set your turkey on top of the sauce; turn to coat both sides. Lock the lid and close the pressure valve. Set to HIGH PRESSURE for 25 minutes.
2. Cancel the KEEP WARM mode and unplug when the timer beeps. NPR for 10 to 15 minutes or till the indicator is down and QPR; unlock the lid and open. Shred the turkey right in the pot using tongs or 2 forks; stir till coated with the sauce. Cover the pot partially; let sits for 5 to 10 minutes to meld the flavors and let the turkey absorb the flavors. Serve.

## Regular Chicken Vindaloo

Servings|**4**   Prep. Time|**10 minutes**   Cook Time|**20 minutes**
**Nut. Content (per serving):** Cal|**242**   Fat|**10g**   Protein|**24g**   Carbs|**12g**

1 carrot, chunked
1 cup florets cauliflower
1 onion (medium), sliced thin
1 pound chicken thighs, boneless & skinless
1 tablespoon garam masala
1 tablespoon garlic & ginger crushed, 3 cloves garlic & 1/2-inch ginger
1 teaspoon salt

1 teaspoon turmeric powder
1/4 cup coconut milk with cream
2 tablespoons cilantro, chopped to garnish
2 teaspoons olive oil, ghee, or butter
3 tablespoons vinegar (red wine)
6 dried whole red chilies, adjust to preference

1. Soak the dried chilies in 1/2 cup of hot water; set aside for 10 minutes. Set the IP to SAUTE. Add the oil. After 30 seconds, add the onion; sauté for 2 minutes or till soft. Turn OFF the IP.
2. Transfer the onions and the rehydrated chilies with the soaking liquid in a blender. Add the coconut milk, salt, spices, ginger, garlic, and vinegar; puree till smooth.
3. Turn ON the IP. Add 1/2 cup water, the spice puree, and the chicken; stir to mix well. Lock the lid and close the pressure valve. Set to HIGH PRESSURE for 6 minutes. NPR when the timer beeps; unlock the lid and open.
4. Add the carrots and cauliflower; stir to mix well. Lock the lid and close the pressure valve. Set to HIGH PRESSURE for 2 minutes. QPR when the timer beeps; unlock the lid and open. Garnish with cilantro. Serve.

## 3-Ingredient Salsa Chicken

Servings|**4**   Prep. Time|**2 minutes**   Cook Time|**8 minutes**
**Nut. Content (per serving):** Cal|**294**   Fat|**5g**   Protein|**49g**   Carbs|**9g**

1 1/3 ounces Taco
1 cup Salsa Autentica
1/4 cup water, adjust depending on the thickness of your salsa

2 pounds (breasts/thighs) chicken, boneless & skinless

1. Turn on the IP. Add the water. Season 1 side of the chicken with 2 to 3 tablespoons of taco seasoning; add them to the pot with the seasoned side beneath. Season the top side with 2 to 3 teaspoons taco seasoning.
2. Mix the salsa with the remaining taco seasoning; pour over the chicken, coating the chicken. Lock the lid and close the pressure valve. Set to HIGH PRESSURE for 8 minutes. NPR for 10 minutes when the timer beeps and QPR; unlock the lid and open.
3. Shred the meat with 2 forks or 2 tongs right in the pot. Stir to mix well. Use for your taco salad, pizza, tortilla soup, quesadillas, enchiladas, or tacos.

# 10-Minute Mediterranean Chicken

Servings|**4**    Prep. Time|**50 minutes**    Cook Time|**10 minutes**
**Nut. Content (per serving):** Cal|**232**    Fat|**8g**    Protein|**36g**    Carbs|**1g**

Spice rub:

1 tablespoon olive oil

1 teaspoon cumin (ground)

1 teaspoon lemon juice

1 teaspoon paprika

1 teaspoon red chili flakes

1 teaspoon salt

1/2 teaspoon black pepper (ground)

1/2 teaspoon garlic powder

1/4 teaspoon cinnamon (ground)

For cooking

1 cup water

1 1/2 pound chicken breasts, boneless & skinless

1. Score the chicken with a knife to allow them to absorb the spice rub. Put all the ingredients in a resealable bag or bowl; mix well. Add the chicken; mix to coat the breasts well. Marinate in the fridge for 30 minutes if possible.

2. Turn ON the IP. Put the IP trivet in the inner pot and pour 1 cup water. Put the chicken o the trivet. Lock the lid and close the pressure valve. Set to HIGH PRESSURE for 6 minutes. NPR when the timer beeps; unlock the lid and open.

3. Transfer the chicken to a cutting board. Let cool for 5 minutes before slicing. Serve with rice, Greek salad, or in a sandwich.

# No-Cream Creamy Chicken

Servings|**6**   Prep. Time|**10 minutes**   Cook Time|**35 minutes**
**Nut. Content (per serving):** Cal|**237**   Fat|**11g**   Protein|**25g**   Carbs|**6g**

Marinade:

1 1/2 pounds chicken thighs or breasts (fat trimmed), boneless & skinless

1 tablespoon garlic & ginger paste, 3 cloves garlic & 1/2-inch ginger

1 teaspoon (1 piece) lime juice

1 teaspoon cumin powder

1 teaspoon garam masala

1 teaspoon salt

1 teaspoon coriander powder

1/2 teaspoon chili powder (red) adjust to preference

1/2 teaspoon turmeric powder

3/4 cup yogurt (plain)

Sauce:

4 tomatoes (medium, ripe) diced, or 14-ounces (canned) diced tomatoes

3 tablespoons yogurt (Greek, plain, full-fat)

2 teaspoon garam masala

2 teaspoon coriander powder

2 tablespoons cilantro, chopped to garnish

12 cashews

1/2 teaspoon chili powder (red) adjust to preference

1 teaspoon turmeric powder

1 teaspoon salt

1 teaspoon paprika (smoked)

1 teaspoon cumin powder

1 tablespoon olive oil

1 tablespoon garlic & ginger paste, 3 cloves garlic & 1/2-inch ginger

1 tablespoon butter or ghee

1 onion (medium), sliced or coarsely chopped

1. Except for the chicken, mix the rest of marinade ingredients in a 1-gallon resealable bag. Add the chicken, seal, and toss to coat well. Marinate in the fridge for 15 minutes or overnight. If short on time, leave while making the sauce.

2. Set the IP to SAUTE. Once HOT, add the oil. Add the marinated chicken; cook for 1 minute each side to seal the flavors. Transfer to a plate; set aside.

3. Sauce: Add the onion, garlic & ginger paste, green chili, and tomato in the pot; sauté for 1 minute. Add the turmeric, paprika, salt, cumin, coriander, and garam masala; sauté for 30 seconds. Add the cashews; stir to mix. Turn OFF the IP. Transfer the mixture to a blender, let cool for 5 minutes, and blend till smooth. Alternatively, puree using an immersion blender right in the pot.

4. Slice the chicken to bite-sized chunks. Add the yogurt to the cooled sauce; blend again. Return the chicken and the sauce in the IP. Add 1/4 cup water (omit if using canned diced tomatoes). Lock the lid and close the pressure valve. Set to HIGH PRESSURE for 6 minutes. NPR for 5 minutes or QPR when the timer beeps; unlock the lid and open. Add 1/2 teaspoon sugar to the dish if using tart tomatoes. Serve garnished with cilantro.

NOTES: If short on time, just dice the chicken. Add to the sauce in the pot and pressure cook the same manner. Add 1 teaspoon more of garam masala to the sauce.

# Pulled Chicken Fajita Tacos

Servings|**8**    Prep. Time|**10 minutes**    Cook Time|**20 minutes**
**Nut. Content (per serving):** Cal|**230**    Fat|**5g**    Protein|**26g**    Carbs|**17g**

1 bell pepper (green), sliced, optional
1 onion (medium), sliced, optional
1 tablespoon olive oil
1 teaspoon cocoa (unsweetened), optional but recommended
1 teaspoon cumin (ground), optional
1 teaspoon paprika (smoked)
1 teaspoon vinegar (red wine)

1/2 teaspoon black pepper
1/2 teaspoon salt
1/4 cup water, use 1/2 cup for a very chunky and thick salsa
12 ounces salsa
2 pounds chicken breast
2 tablespoons chili powder (Mexican)
8 tortillas (corn)

1. Set the IP to SAUTE. After 30 seconds, add the oil, bell peppers, and onion; sauté for 30 seconds. Add the vinegar; sauté for 30 seconds. Add 1/4 teaspoon pepper and 1/4 teaspoon salt; stir to mix well. Transfer the mixture to a bowl; set aside to keep them crunchy, or leave them in the pot and cook with the chicken.

2. Turn OFF the IP. Mix the spices and the salsa. Add the water and chicken in the pot. Pour the salsa over them to cover with the sauce. Lock the lid and close the pressure valve. Set to HIGH PRESSURE for 8 minutes or for 10 minutes for thick breasts.

3. NPR for 10 minutes when the timer beeps and QPR; unlock the lid and open. Transfer the chicken to a platter; shred using 2 forks. Mix the cocoa in the sauce till well mixed. Add the shredded chicken and the pepper mixture in the pot; stir to mix well. Serve with warmed tortillas and preferred topping, like jalapenos, salsa, sour cream, and cheese.

# Authentic Butter Chicken

Servings | **4**     Prep. Time | **30 minutes**     Cook Time | **30 minutes**
**Nut. Content (per serving):** Cal | **342**     Fat | **22g**     Protein | **26g**     Carbs | **8g**

Marinade:
1 pound chicken (breasts or thighs),
boneless & skinless, fat-trimmed, cubed in
2-inch chunks
1 tablespoon garlic & ginger paste, 3 cloves
garlic & 1/2-inch ginger
1 teaspoon coriander powder
1 teaspoon garam masala
1 teaspoon paprika
1/2 cup yogurt (plain Greek)
1/2 teaspoon salt
1/2 teaspoon turmeric powder
1/4 teaspoon chili powder (red) or cayenne
2 teaspoon olive oil
Juice of 1/2 a lime

Sauce:
1 tablespoon ghee olive oil
14 ounces (canned) diced tomatoes or 4 to
5 tomatoes (ripe), pureed
1 tablespoon garlic & ginger paste, 3 cloves
garlic & 1/2-inch ginger
1/2 teaspoon salt adjust to preference
1/2 teaspoon turmeric powder
1/4 teaspoon chili powder (red) or cayenne
2 teaspoons garam masala
2 teaspoons coriander powder
1 teaspoon cumin powder
1 teaspoon paprika
1 teaspoon sugar (white or brown), optional

After cooking:
1/2 cup cream (heavy whipping) or coconut
cream
1 tablespoon cilantro, chopped to garnish

1. Marinade the chicken (optional, but recommended): If not marinating add 1 teaspoon garam masala in your sauce. Mix all of the marinade ingredients. Add the chicken and coat well. Refrigerate for 30 minutes to marinate, or up to overnight.
2. Mix all of the sauce ingredients in the pot. Add the marinated chicken. Lock the lid and close the pressure valve. Set to HIGH PRESSURE for 6 minutes. NPR when the timer beeps; unlock the lid and open. Add the cream (heavy). Serve garnished with cilantro together with cumin rice or naan.

## Kung Pao Tofu or Chicken

Servings | **4**    Prep. Time | **10 minutes**    Cook Time | **10 minutes**
**Nut. Content (per serving):** Cal | **248**    Fat | **7g**    Protein | **28g**    Carbs | **17g**

Sauce:
1 tablespoon sambal oelek
1 tablespoon vinegar (rice)
1 teaspoon cornstarch
1-2 tablespoons honey
2 teaspoons hoisin sauce
3 tablespoons soy sauce (low-sodium)
3 tablespoons water

Main ingredients:
1 cup (2 stalks) celery, chopped
1 cup florets broccoli, optional
1 cup zucchini (1 piece) or carrots (2 pieces), chopped
1 pound chicken breast or thigh (boneless & skinless), sliced into 1-inch chunks, or 1 cup tofu (extra firm), cut into 1/2-inch cubes
1 small bell pepper (red), sliced in 1/2-inch pieces
1 teaspoon garlic, grated or chopped finely
1 teaspoon ginger, grated or chopped finely
1/2 onions, sliced into quarters
1/2 teaspoon sesame oil, for finishing
2 tablespoons peanuts (roasted unsalted), for finishing

1. Prepare the veggies. Mix all the sauce ingredients till smooth. Chop the tofu or chicken.
2. Set the IP to SAUTE MORE mode. Once your cooker says HOT, add your garlic and our ginger, cook for around 15 seconds. Add the chicken; sauté for 3 to 4 minutes or till almost cooked. Add the veggies (and tofu if using instead of chicken); sauté for 3 to 4 minutes. Once the chicken is done; stir the sauce and add in the pot; stir to coat the chicken (tofu) and veggies. Add the sesame oil; stir to coat. Turn off the SAUTE. Add the peanuts. Serve over brown or white Jasmine rice.
NOTES: You can also cook the veggies and chicken using HIGH PRESSURE for 1 minute. QPR when the timer beeps; unlock the lid and open. Add the sauce and cook using SAUTE mode till mixed.

# White Chicken Chili

Servings|**6**    Prep. Time|**10 minutes**    Cook Time|**15 minutes**
**Nut. Content (per serving):** Cal|**303**    Fat|**8g**    Protein|**28g**    Carbs|**28g**

1 cup celery, washed & chopped or sliced, around 2 ribs
1 cup corn (frozen)
1 garlic, crushed, or 1/2 teaspoon garlic powder
1 pound chicken tenders, thighs, or breasts, boneless & skinless, omit for vegetarian
1 tablespoon olive oil (extra-virgin)
1 teaspoon cumin (ground)
1 teaspoon salt
1/4 cup cheddar cheese, shredded, around 1 tablespoon per serving, or preferred chili toppings

1/4 to 1/2 teaspoon cayenne pepper optional
14 ounces (canned) Northern beans, rinsed & drained
2 cups kale, washed & chopped, optional
2 teaspoons chili powder
2 to 3 tablespoons cilantro, chopped, to garnish
32-ounce stock (chicken or vegetable)
A couple drops lime juice, before serving

1. Put everything in the IP; stir to mix well. Lock the lid and close the pressure valve. Set to HIGH PRESSURE for 4 minutes for tenders. Set for 6 to 7 minutes for chicken breasts chopped small or thighs sliced in half; shred later. Set for 6 minutes for whole thighs; shred later.
2. NPR for 10 minutes when the timer beeps and QPR; unlock the lid and open. Shred the chicken using 2 forks or tongs right in the pot. Drizzle with lime juice and garnish with preferred chili toppings, such as tortilla chips, sour cream, cheese, and cilantro.

## Ethiopian Chicken Noodle Soup

Servings|**6**    Prep. Time|**10 minutes**    Cook Time|**10 minutes**
**Nut. Content (per serving):** Cal|**175**    Fat|**5g**    Protein|**20g**    Carbs|**11g**

1 cup carrots, chopped
1 cup celery, chopped
1 pound chicken breast
1 tablespoon olive oil
1 tablespoon Sriracha or tomato paste for a milder heat
1 teaspoon salt adjust to preference

1/2 cup elbow pasta (whole-grain)
2 garlic cloves, crushed
2 to 3 teaspoon Berbere seasoning adjust to preference
32 ounces broth (chicken or vegetable), low-sodium

1. Set the IP to SAUTE. After 30 seconds, add the olive oil and garlic; let sizzle for 30 seconds. Add the carrots and celery. Add everything else; mix well. Cancel SAUTE. Lock the lid and close the pressure valve. Set to HIGH PRESSURE for 6 to 8 minutes.
2. NPR for 10 minutes when the timer beeps and QPR; unlock the lid and open. Remove the poultry to a wooden board; shred the meat. Return the chicken in the pot. Serve garnished with cilantro.

## Keto Chicken Vindaloo

Servings|**4**    Prep. Time|**10 minutes**    Cook Time|**20 minutes**
**Nut. Content (per serving):** Cal|**206**    Fat|**7g**    Protein|**23g**    Carbs|**10g**

1 onion (medium), sliced thin
1 pound chicken thighs, boneless & skinless
1 tablespoon garam masala
1 tablespoon garlic & ginger crushed, 3 cloves garlic & 1/2-inch ginger
1 teaspoon salt
1 teaspoon turmeric powder

1/4 cup coconut milk with cream
2 tablespoons cilantro, chopped to garnish
2 teaspoons olive oil, ghee, or butter
3 tablespoons vinegar (red wine)
6 dried whole red chilies, adjust to preference

1. Soak the dried chilies in 1/2 cup of hot water; set aside for 10 minutes. Set the IP to SAUTE. Add the oil. After 30 seconds, add the onion; sauté for 2 minutes or till soft. Turn OFF the IP.
2. Transfer the onions and the rehydrated chilies with the soaking liquid in a blender. Add the coconut milk, salt, spices, ginger, garlic, and vinegar; puree till smooth.
3. Turn ON the IP. Add 1/2 cup water, the spice puree, and the chicken; stir to mix well. Lock the lid and close the pressure valve. Set to HIGH PRESSURE for 6 minutes. NPR when the timer beeps; unlock the lid and open. Serve with French bread (toasted) or steamed rice.

# Jamaican Jerk Chicken

Servings | **4**    Prep. Time | **30 minutes**    Cook Time | **25 minutes**
**Nut. Content (per serving):** Cal | **203**    Fat | **7g**    Protein | **25g**    Carbs | **8g**

1 pound chicken (thighs or breasts), skinless & boneless

Marinade:
1 packed tablespoon sugar (brown)
1 tablespoon olive oil (light)
1 tablespoon soy sauce
1/2 inch ginger grated or crushed
2 cloves garlic chopped finely, or 1/4 teaspoon garlic powder
2 tablespoon seasoning (Caribbean Jerk)
2 to 3 tablespoons thinly sliced spring onions
3 tablespoons orange juice
3 tablespoons vinegar (red wine) or vinegar (apple cider)

Jerk seasoning mix (makes 2 tablespoons):
1 teaspoon red pepper (crushed), adjust to preference
1 teaspoon thyme (dried)
1/2 teaspoon allspice
1/2 teaspoon black pepper
1/2 teaspoon garlic powder
1/2 teaspoon ginger (ground)
1/2 teaspoon salt
1/4 teaspoon cinnamon (ground)
1/4 teaspoon cloves (ground)

1. Mix all the marinade ingredients in a mixing bowl (small). Transfer the mixture a 1-gallon resealable bag. Add the chicken, remove as much air as possible and seal. Turn the bag a couple of times to coat well. If possible, marinate in the fridge for 30 minutes up to 12 hours.
2. Turn ON the IP. Add the chicken and the marinade. Lock the lid and close the pressure valve. Set to HIGH PRESSURE for 6 minutes for thighs or for 6 to 8 minutes for breasts. NPR for 10 minutes when the timer beeps and QPR; unlock the lid and open.
3. Transfer the chicken to a plate; let rest. Set the IP to SAUTE, let come to a simmer. Cook for 3 to 5 minutes or till the sauce is thick.
4. Optional step: Heat your grill pan over medium-high flame/heat. Put the chicken on the pan with the presentation side under. Cook for 30 to 60 seconds or till gorgeous grill marks appear. Drizzle the sauce over the chicken. Serve with a side of veggies, potato, or rice.

# Tandoori Chicken Sliders

Servings|**8**   Prep. Time|**10 minutes**   Cook Time|**12 minutes**
**Nut. Content (per serving):** Cal|**339**   Fat|**20g**   Protein|**18g**   Carbs|**19g**

1 1/2 pounds chicken thighs, extra-fat trimmed, skinless & boneless

Marinade:
1 tablespoon coriander (ground)
1 tablespoon garam masala
1 tablespoon ginger (1/2-inch) & garlic (3 cloves), grated or crushed
1 teaspoon salt
1 teaspoon turmeric (ground)
1/2 cup Yogurt (Greek) or 3/4 cup yogurt (regular plain)
1/4 teaspoon cayenne pepper adjust to preference
2 tablespoons olive oil (light)
2 teaspoons (around 1/2 lime) lime juice
2 teaspoons paprika or chili powder (Kashmiri red)

Garnish
1 teaspoon lime juice (fresh) drizzled on top
1/2 teaspoon Chaat Masala, to season the chicken lightly, optional

Sliders:
1 onion, thinly sliced
4 cups lettuce (green butter & purple)
8 slider buns
8 tablespoon cilantro chutney spread (spread 1 tablespoon per slider)

Cilantro chutney:
1 tablespoon honey, optional, but recommended
1/2 teaspoon chaat masala
1/2 teaspoon ground cumin (roasted)
1/2 teaspoon salt, adjust to preference
1/4 cup water, adjust to preference
1-inch ginger (fresh), peeled
2 cups cilantro, washed & drained
2 green chilies, slice off the tops
1 lime, juice only (around 1 1/2 to 2 tablespoons)

1. In a resealable bag (large) or a mixing bowl, mix all the marinade ingredients till well combined. Add the chicken, close the bag if using. Toss to coat the pieces well with the marinade. Refrigerate for at least 30 minutes or overnight.
2. Put the IP trivet in the inner pot and pour 1 cup water. Put the chicken on the trivet. Lock the lid and close the pressure valve. Set to HIGH PRESSURE for 6 minutes. NPR for 5 minutes when the timer beeps and QPR; unlock the lid and open. Transfer the chicken to a sheet pan. Broil for 2 to 3 minutes or till crisp.
3. Cilantro chutney: Trim 2-inch odd the ends of the cilantro stem. Wash 2 to 3 times. Drain well. Put the ginger, chilies, water, and lime juice in a blender; blend till smooth. Add the cilantro and the rest of the ingredients in the blender; blend for 30 seconds. Adjust consistency and seasoning as needed. Store in the fridge for up to 1 week.
4. Chutney spread: Mix the chutney and yogurt till combined. Spread around 1 tablespoon of the mixture on each bun halves. Add the chicken, lettuce, and onion. Top with the bun. Serve.

# Prosciutto Chicken Breast Rolls

Servings | **6**   Prep. Time | **5 minutes**   Cook Time | **10 minutes**
**Nut. Content (per serving):** Cal | **394.5**   Fat | **13 1/2g**   Protein | **58.3g**   Carbs | **5.1g**

1 cup peas (frozen), not extra-small or petite
1 tablespoon butter
1 tablespoon olive oil
1 teaspoon salt

1/4 cup wine (dry white)
10 sage leaves (large)
3/4 cup stock (chicken)
6 chicken breasts
6 prosciutto slices

1. Place the meat between sheets of wax paper; pound into a relatively even thinness. Lay them so that the more square side is away from you. Cover each piece with the prosciutto, matching them with the top of the breast. If the prosciutto is longer, bunch them to reach the side of the breast close to you; roll each piece tightly fasten the chicken roll securely using a small skewer or a toothpick while spearing a sage leaf into each roll.
2. Set the IP to SAUTE. Once, HOT, add the oil and the rest of the sage. Set the IP to SAUTE MORE mode. Working in batches, place the chicken with the sage leaf under in the pot; cook till brown.
3. Once all the rolls are brown, set them in the IP with the sage leaf above. Add the wine, pouring it around the chicken. Let the wine evaporate completely. Add the stock and salt if using. Pour the peas on top of the rolls.
4. Lock the lid and close the pressure valve. Set to HIGH PRESSURE for 5 minutes. QPR when the timer beeps; unlock the lid and open. Serve with a good scoop of peas and the cooking liquid. Great with creamy polenta or mashed potatoes.

## Spicy Buffalo Chicken Wings

Servings | **24**    Prep. Time | **5 minutes**    Cook Time | **25 minutes**
**Nut. Content (per serving):** Cal | **94**    Fat | **3g**    Protein | **11.7g**    Carbs | **4.5g**

1 pound celery, trimmed
2 pounds (1 kilogram) chicken wings
(around 12 pieces), cut at the joint to make
around 24 pieces

For the dipping sauce:
1 tablespoon parsley
1 cup (250milliliters) milk yogurt (plain
whole)

Coating:
1/4 cup honey
1/4 cup tomato puree
3 teaspoons salt
4 tablespoons hot sauce

1. Put the IP steamer basket in the inner pot and pour 1 cup water. Put the chicken in the basket, placing them vertically on their ends as needed. Lock the lid and close the pressure valve. Set to HIGH PRESSURE for 10 minutes.
2. While the chicken is cooking, put the coating ingredients in a bowl (large) and mix well using a fork till the honey it dissolved completely.
3. QPR when the timer beeps; unlock the lid and open. Transfer the chicken to the bowl with coating; coat well and evenly. Transfer the coated chicken in a baking sheet lined with parchment paper. Broil for 5 minutes or till crisp and brown. Meanwhile, prepare a serving plate with the sauce and celery sticks. Brush the crispy chicken with the remaining sauce and transfer to the serving plate.

## Easy Butter Chicken

Servings | **4**     Prep. Time | **20 minutes**     Cook Time | **30-35 minutes**
**Nut. Content (per serving):** Cal | **300.9**     Fat | **17.1g**     Protein | **30.3g**     Carbs | **5.1g**

1 1/2 cups (14 1/2 ounces) crushed tomatoes (canned)
1 cup stock (chicken) or water
1 red onion (small), sliced
1 tablespoon ginger (fresh) or 1 teaspoon powdered
1 teaspoon salt
1/3 cup cream (heavy)

2 pounds (1 kilogram) chicken breasts (frozen), around 4 pieces
2 tablespoons butter or preferred, divided
2 tablespoons garam masala, divided
3 cloves garlic, finely minced
3 sprigs coriander, chopped finely, to garnish
3 tablespoons tomato paste or concentrate

1. Set the IP to SAUTE. Once HOT, add 1 tablespoon butter/oil. Once starting to sizzle, add the onion; sauté for 4 minutes or till soft, stirring occasionally. Add the ginger, salt, 1 tablespoon garam masala; stir to mix well. Add the stock.
2. In a single layer, arrange the chicken in the pot, placing them vertically as needed. Spread the tomato paste on top of the poultry. Add the crushed tomatoes. DO NOT STIR. Season the rest of the garam masala on top. DO NOT STIR.
3. Lock the lid and close the pressure valve. Set to HIGH PRESSURE for 5 to 7 minutes for frozen or for 3 minutes for unfrozen chicken. NPR when the timer beeps; unlock the lid and open. Carefully mix in the rest of the butter, cream, and garlic, wiggling and lifting the chicken carefully in the process.
4. The internal temperature of the poultry should be at least 165F before serving. If desired, you can puree the cooking juices for a smoother texture. Serve over Quinoa & Rice or cooked Basmati Rice.

## Cornish Game Hen

Servings | **1-2**    Prep. Time | **10 minutes**    Cook Time | **12 minutes**
**Nut. Content (per serving):** Cal | **663.5**    Fat | **46.15g**    Protein | **40g**    Carbs | **23g**

1 lemon (small), cut in eighths, divided in half
1 piece (2 pounds) Cornish rock or game hen
1 sprig rosemary, thyme, or both (fresh), optional
1 tablespoon cooking oil
1 teaspoon garlic powder
1 teaspoon poultry seasoning
1 teaspoon salt

1/2 onion (small), sliced
1/3 cup water
1/4 teaspoon pepper
2 potatoes (small), halved, leave whole if very small & pierce using a fork, optional
2 tablespoons butter, softened

Gravy:
2 to 3 tablespoons butter, softened
2 to 3 tablespoons flour (all-purpose)

1. Dry the hen using paper towels. Rub the out the under the skin with the butter. Season with the pepper, salt, garlic powder, and poultry seasoning; sprinkle the cavity with the seasoning as well. Loosely stuff the cavity with the rosemary and lemon wedges.
2. Set the IP to SAUTE. Once HOT, add the oil. With the breast side under, put the hen in the pot; cook for 3 minutes undisturbed. With tongs, flip and cook the other side for 3 minutes. Transfer the hen to a plate. Add the onion to the pot; cook for a couple of minutes, stirring and scraping the brown bits off the pot. Add the water; stir to mix.
3. With the breast side above, return the hen in the pot. Add the optional potatoes. Cancel SAUTE. Squeeze the juice of the remaining lemon in the pot. Lock the lid and close the pressure valve. Set to MANUAL HIGH PRESSURE for 12 minutes. NPR for 10 minutes when the timer beeps and QPR; unlock the lid and open.
4. Using tongs, transfer the hen to a baking sheet if broiling or to a plate if otherwise. If broiling, turn the broiler on to 400F. Broil the hen till browned to preference. Serve right away if not broiling.
5. Gravy: Set the IP to SAUTÉ. Remove the onion from the pot using a slotted spoon if you do not like them in the gravy. Mix the butter and flour to create a paste. Add to the pot; stir till thick. Turn the pot off. Serve the gravy over the hen and potatoes.

# Butter Chicken

Servings | **2**    Prep. Time | **10 minutes**    Cook Time | **10minutes**
**Nut. Content (per serving):** Cal | **657**    Fat | **27g**    Protein | **68g**    Carbs | **25.7g**

1 tablespoon cornstarch
1 teaspoon cumin (ground)
1 teaspoon garam masala
1 teaspoon paprika (smoked)
1 teaspoon turmeric
1 yellow onion (small), diced
1/2 bell pepper (red), diced
1/2 teaspoon salt
1/3 cup cream (heavy)

14-ounce (canned) tomato sauce
1-inch ginger, peeled
2 cloves garlic
2 tablespoons butter (unsalted)
4 chicken thighs (boneless, skinless), fat trimmed, cubed into 2-inch pieces
Rice (Basmati) (cooked), to serve
Cilantro (fresh), to serve
Pinch cayenne pepper, optional

1. Set the IP to SAUTE. Add the butter; let melt. Add the onion and bell pepper; stir to goat. With a microplane, grate the ginger and garlic into the pot; stir to mix. Add the salt, paprika, turmeric, and garam masala; stir to mix. Add 1 dash of cayenne as desired.  Stir to mix very well.
2. Turn off the IP. Add the tomato sauce and chicken in the pot.; stir to mix and coat. Set the IP to HIGH PRESSURE for 10 minutes. Lock the lid and close the pressure valve.
3. QPR when the timer beeps; unlock the lid and open. While the pressure is releasing, whisk the cornstarch and the cream (heavy) to mix very well. Add to the IP; stir to mix well and let thicken with the residual heat. Serve over cooked rice, top with cilantro, and if desired, with warm naan bread. If you have time, brush the naan bread with butter and garlic.

# PASTA & NOODLES

## Noodle Chicken Soup

Servings|**3**    Prep. Time|**10 minutes**    Cook Time|**33 minutes**
**Nut. Content (per serving):** Cal|**419**    Fat|**17.7g**    Protein|**25.2g**    Carbs|**12.1g**

1 1/2 sprigs thyme (fresh)
1 garlic cloves, peeled
1 sprig fresh sage
1 tablespoon olive oil
1/2 red onion (medium), peeled & halved
1/2 tablespoon dill fronds (fresh), chopped finely
1/4 teaspoon black pepper (ground)

1/4 teaspoon salt (table), adjust to preference
2 carrots (medium), peeled & cut to fit the pot
2 chicken thighs, bone-in & skinless, (8 ounces each)
2 ounces (no-yolk or egg) wide noodles
3 cups broth (chicken)

1. Set the IP to SAUTE for 15 minutes. Add the oil; heat for 1 to 2 minutes. Meanwhile, season the chicken with the pepper and salt. Put them in the pot; cook for 6 minutes or till brown, flipping a few times. Transfer to a bowl.

2. Add the broth in the pot. Press CANCEL. Scrape the brown bits off the IP. Add the chicken, sage, thyme, garlic, carrots, and onion. Lock the lid and close the pressure valve. Set to HIGH PRESSURE for 18 minutes. QPR when the timer beeps; unlock the lid and open.

3. Transfer the chicken to a slicing board (large). With a slotted spoon, remove the herbs and veggies from the pot. Stir the dill and the noodles in the broth. Lock the lid and close the pressure valve. Set to HIGH PRESSURE for 4 minutes.

4. Meanwhile, remove the tough cartilage and any bones from the meat and discard. Slice the meat into spoon-sized chunks. QPR when the timer beeps; unlock the lid and open. Stir the meat in the pot; adjust salt as needed.

## Dan Dan Noodles

Servings|**2**    Prep. Time|**5 minutes**    Cook Time|**16 minutes**
**Nut. Content (per serving):** Cal|**557**    Fat|**21g**    Protein|**42.8g**    Carbs|**48.9g**

1 1/2 medium cloves garlic, peeled & minced (1/2 tablespoon)
1 1/2 tablespoon vinegar (balsamic)
1 cups broth (chicken)
1 tablespoon dry vermouth, dry sherry, or water
1 tablespoon honey
1 tablespoon pepper sauce (hot red or sambal oelek, such as Sriracha), adjust to preference

1 tablespoon preferred cooking oil
1/2 pound lean ground pork
1/2 tablespoon ginger (fresh), peeled & minced
1/2 tablespoon Worcestershire sauce
1/8 cup soy sauce
1/8 cup tahini
3 scallions (medium), trimmed & thinly sliced
4 ounces spaghetti (dried), break into half

1. Set the IP to SAUTE for 10 minutes. Add the oil; let heat for 1 to 2 minutes. Crumble the meat, add to the pot, and cook for 4 minutes or till gray but not brown, breaking any clumps and stirring often. Stir in the ginger, garlic, hot sauce, and scallions; cook for a couple of seconds.
2. Add the Worcestershire, sherry, honey, vinegar, soy sauce, and tahini; stir to mix well. Press CANCEL. Add the spaghetti; submerge them in the sauce without touching the base of the pot.
3. Lock the lid and close the pressure valve. Set to HIGH PRESSURE for 6 minutes. QPR when the timer beeps; unlock the lid and open. Stir to mix well. Serve.

## Mac & Cheese

Servings|**2 to 3**    Prep. Time|**10 minutes**    Cook Time|**10 minutes**
**Nut. Content (per 3 servings):** Cal|**301**    Fat|**11.2g**    Protein|**19.1g**    Carbs|**30.1g**

1 cup broth (vegetable)
1 ounce Parmesan cheese, grated (1/4 cup)
1 tablespoon butter (unsalted)
1/4 teaspoon garlic powder

2 tablespoons sour cream
4 ounces cheddar (extra-sharp), grated
4 ounces macaroni noodles (around 1 cup)

1. Put the macaroni, broth, garlic powder, and butter in the IP; stir to mix well. Lock the lid and close the pressure valve. Set to HIGH PRESSURE for 5 minutes. While the IP cooks the noodles, prepare the rest of the ingredients.
2. QPR when the timer beeps; unlock the lid and open. Add the rest of the ingredients; stir to mix and let rest for 5 minutes. The mixture should be smooth and. Otherwise, Set the IP to KEEP WARM to heat the mixture till everything is melted. Serve right away. Reheat leftovers with 1 splash of milk.

## Minestrone Macaroni Pesto Soup

Servings|**3**   Prep. Time|**10 minutes**   Cook Time|**8 minutes**
**Nut. Content (per serving):** Cal|**242**   Fat|**10.9g**   Protein|**15.6g**   Carbs|**23.9g**

1 1/2 medium cloves garlic, peeled & minced (1 tablespoon)
1 carrot (medium), chopped (1/2 cup)
1 celery ribs (medium), chopped (1/3 cup)
1 ounce elbow macaroni (gluten-free or whole-wheat)
1 ounce Parmigiano-Reggiano, finely grated (1 cup)
1/2 onion (medium yellow), chopped (1/2 cup)
1/2 teaspoon salt (table)
1/2 zucchini (medium, around 3 ounces), halved lengthwise & sliced thinly into half-moons, or 3 ounces spiraled

1/4 cup walnuts, roughly chopped
1/4 loosely packed cup basil leaves (fresh), chopped
1/4 teaspoon flakes red pepper
2 red tomatoes (large round), chopped (2 cups)
3 cups broth (vegetable)
7 1/2 ounces (canned) beans, drained & rinsed
1/2 tablespoon sugar (granulated white), to sweeten a bit, optional

1. Mix the beans, broth, red pepper, salt, garlic, walnuts, basil, zucchini, celery, carrots, onion, and tomatoes in the IP. Stir in the pasta. Set to HIGH PRESSURE for 8 minutes. Cancel the KEEP WARM mode and unplug when the timer beeps. NPR for 10 to 15 minutes or till the indicator is down and QPR; unlock the lid and open.
2. Stir in the cheese; cover partially with the lid and let sit for 5 minutes to meld the flavors. Serve each bowl with a drizzle of aromatic, fine olive oil.

# Wonton Chicken Soup

Servings | **4**    Prep. Time | **10 minutes**    Cook Time | **10 minutes**
**Nut. Content (per serving):** Cal | **373**    Fat | **9g**    Protein | **14g**    Carbs | **63g**

1 pack mini wontons (frozen)
1 tablespoon chili garlic paste (ground fresh), o preferred chili garlic sauce
1 tablespoon fish sauce, optional
1 tablespoon vinegar (rice)
1 teaspoon honey or agave nectar
1/2 teaspoon sesame oil (roasted)
1/2-inch ginger, peeled & chopped finely, or 1/2 teaspoon ginger (ground)

2 cloves garlic peeled & chopped finely, or 1/2 teaspoon garlic powder
2 tablespoons soy sauce (low-sodium), or as needed
2 to 3 heads bok choy, greens (leaves) & stems separated, chopped
3 carrots (medium), sliced
32 ounces (packed) chicken or vegetable stock

1.  Turn ON the IP. Except for the wontons, and bok choy leaves, add the rest of the ingredients in the pot. Lock the lid and close the pressure valve. Set to HIGH PRESSURE for 2 minutes. QPR when the timer beeps; unlock the lid and open.
2. Set the IP to SAUTE. Add the wonton; cook for 2 to 4 minutes or till they float on top. Cancel SAUTE. Add the bok choy leaves; stir to mix and wait for the leaves to soften. Serve.

# Mac & Cheese

Servings | **3 cups**    Prep. Time | **10 minutes**    Cook Time | **4 minutes**
**Nut. Content (per serving):** Cal | **560**    Fat | **25.2g**    Protein | **23g**    Carbs | **59.2g**

1 cup cheddar cheese (sharp), shredded
1/4 teaspoon salt
1/4 teaspoon seasoned salt
2 cups broth (chicken) or water
2 tablespoons butter
2/3 cup cream (heavy), evaporated milk, or milk or evaporated milk
8 ounces (around 2 cups) elbow macaroni (small)
Pinch pepper

Optional (add to the pot before pressure-cooking:
1/2 teaspoon mustard (ground)
2 to 3 dashes hot sauce, add before cooking

1. Set the IP to SAUTE. Add the broth or water. Add the salt, pepper, seasoned salt, butter, and optional flavorings. Stir and let come to a simmer. Stir in the macaroni.
2. Lock the lid and close the pressure valve. Cancel SAUTÉ. Set to MANUAL HIGH PRESSURE for 4 minutes. QPR in short bursts when the timer beeps; unlock the lid and open. Stir the pasta mixture. If there is too much liquid, scoop out some of it and reserve. Add the cheese; stir well till melted. Stir in the cream and milk. Adjust seasoning as needed. Let sit for a couple minutes to thicken. If it is too thick, stir some of the reserved cooking liquid, milk, or cream in the pot.

## Thai Red Curry Soup

Servings|4    Prep. Time|**10 minutes**    Cook Time|**20 minutes**
**Nut. Content (per serving):** Cal|**484**    Fat|**19g**    Protein|**32g**    Carbs|**49g**

Pressure cooking:
1 pound chicken (thighs or breasts), skinless & boneless, chunked to 1-inch pieces
1 stalk lemongrass, sliced into 3 to 4 pieces
1 tablespoon olive oil (light)
1/2 a bunch cilantro, added as is
1/2 inch ginger, ground or grated, or 1/4 teaspoon ginger (ground)
1/2 teaspoon salt adjust to preference
2 cloves garlic, ground or grated, or 1/4 teaspoon garlic powder
2 tablespoons curry paste (Maesri Thai red), adjust to preference
2 tablespoons fish sauce, omit for vegetarian/vegan
3 cups broth (chicken or vegetable)

After pressure-cooking:
1 can baby corn, rinsed &drained
1 carrot (around 1/2 cup, sliced in half-moons
1 onion (small) sliced (around 1/2 cup)
1 small bell pepper sliced (around 1/2 cup)
1 to 2 tablespoons sugar or honey (adjust to preference)
1 zucchini (around 1/2 cup), sliced in half-moons
1/2 can coconut milk, stirred well before adding
1/2 cup basil leaves (fresh Thai)
2 ounces brown rice (Pad Thai) noodles, around 1/4 box

Garnish:
2 tablespoons cilantro (fresh), chopped
1/2 lime, juiced

1. Prepare the meat and veggies before cooking. Set the IP to SAUTE. Add the oil. Once heated, add the chicken, garlic, ginger, and curry paste; sauté for 30 to 45 seconds. Add the broth and the rest of the ingredients for pressure-cooking; stir to mix well. Cancel SAUTE. Lock the lid and close the pressure valve. Set to HIGH PRESSURE for 5 minutes. QPR gradually when the timer beeps; unlock the lid and open.

2. Remove the cilantro bunch from the pot. Add the noodles, basil, coconut milk, and veggies in the pot. Set the IP to SAUTE; cook for 3 to 4 minutes or till the noodles are cooked through. Add the lime juice and honey. Remove the lemongrass. Serve garnished with cilantro.

# Chicken Noodle Soup

Servings | **6**    Prep. Time | **10 minutes**    Cook Time | **16 minutes**
**Nut. Content (per serving):** Cal | **200**    Fat | **6g**    Protein | **14g**    Carbs | **20g**

1 1/4 teaspoons salt

1 onion (medium) chopped or sliced

1 pound chicken (breast/thighs/drums), skinless or skin-on, bone-in

1 tablespoon olive oil

1 teaspoon (around 1/2 small piece) lemon juice

1/2 teaspoon oregano

1/2 teaspoon thyme (dried)

2 bay leaves

2 cups (2 stalks) celery, sliced

2 cups carrots (baby), sliced into halves

2 tablespoon parsley, chopped

2 teaspoons (2 cloves) garlic, chopped finely

2 teaspoons (1/2-inch) ginger chopped finely

2 teaspoons coriander (ground)

2 to 4 ounces noodles (brown rice)

3/4 teaspoon black pepper (crushed)

4 cups stock (chicken) or water

1. Remove the skin from the chicken or leave them on. Set the IP to SAUTE. Add the oil. Once heated, add the ginger, veggies, and garlic; sauté for 30 seconds. Add the chicken, stock, spices, and bay leaves; stir to mix well. Lock the lid and close the pressure valve. Set to SOUP or MANUAL for 10 minutes. NPR for 5 minutes when the timer beeps and QPR; unlock the lid and open.

2. Transfer the chicken to a slicing board; shred the meat. Set the IP to SAUTE. Add the noodles and let come to a simmer; cook for 5 to6 minutes or till the noodles are done. Add the chicken meat and lime juice. Serve warm.

NOTES: If using water instead of stock, add 1/2 teaspoon black pepper, 1/2 teaspoon salt, and 1/2 teaspoon oregano.

# Pasta Minestrone Soup

Servings|**4 -6**    Prep. Time|**5 minutes**    Cook Time|**20 minutes**
**Nut. Content (per 6 servings):** Cal|**218.5**    Fat|**3.3g**    Protein|**4.7g**    Carbs|**22.4g**

For pressure-cooking:
1 bay leaf
1 carrot, chopped
1 celery stalk, chopped
1 cup (250milliliters) dry chickpeas, quick-soaked or soaked overnight
1 garlic clove, finely minced
1 onion, chopped
1 sprig rosemary
1 sprig sage
1 tablespoon olive oil
2 tablespoons tomato puree or passata, or
1 tablespoon tomato concentrate
4 cups (1 liter) water

After cooking:
1 1/2 teaspoons salt
1 cup Ditalini or preferred medium-small pasta
1/4 teaspoon pepper
3 cups (750milliliters) water

1. Set the IP to SAUTE. Once HOT, add the oil, celery, carrot, and onion; sauté till soft. Add the herbs; stir for 1 minute. Add the chickpeas, water, and tomato puree. Lock the lid and close the pressure valve. Set to HIGH PRESSURE for 18 minutes. Cancel the KEEP WARM mode and unplug when the timer beeps. NPR for 10 to 15 minutes or till the indicator is down and QPR; unlock the lid and open.

2. Discard the bay leaf and the woody stems of the herbs. Add 3 cups of water. Season with pepper and salt. Set the IP to SAUTE; let come to a boil. Once boiling, add the pasta; cook following package instructions. Serve with optional Pecorino Romano.

# Tortellini Soup

Servings | **5 cups**    Prep. Time | **15 minutes**    Cook Time | **5 minutes**
**Nut. Content (per serving):** Cal | **206**    Fat | **6.2g**    Protein | **20.9g**    Carbs | **15.6g**

1 bay leaf
1 cup mushrooms, thickly sliced
1 cup tortellini (refrigerated)
1 sprig rosemary (fresh), around 3 to 4-inch long
1 sprig thyme (fresh) or 1/2 teaspoon dried
1 teaspoon ginger (fresh), grated or 1/4 teaspoon powdered
1/2 pound ground lean beef or turkey, preferably 97% lean
1/2 sweet onion (small), chopped
1/2 teaspoon kosher or 1/4 teaspoon salt (table)

1/4 teaspoon pepper
15 ounces (canned) white beans, drained & rinsed
2 carrots (small), chopped
2 cloves garlic (small), finely minced or pressed
3 1/4 cups broth (chicken or vegetable), preferably low-sodium

Optional:
3/4 cup sweet potato, cubed
Garnish
Parmesan cheese, grated

1. Set the IP to SAUTE NORMAL mode. Once HOT, add the meat (add a bit of oil if using turkey); cook till almost done, stirring occasionally. Add the onion and carrots, stir and cook for a couple of minutes till the onions start to turn translucent. Add the ginger and garlic; stir to mix. Add the broth; stir to mix. Add the beans, sweet potato, pepper, salt, mushrooms, rosemary, thyme, and bay leaf. Stir in the tortellini.
2. Lock the lid and close the pressure valve. Cancel SAUTE. Set to MANUAL HIGH PRESSURE for 5 minutes. NPR for 5 minutes when the timer beeps and QPR; unlock the lid and open. Stir the soup. Adjust seasoning as needed. Serve garnish as desired.
NOTES: Omit the meat and use vegetable broth to make this vegetarian.

# Spaghetti

Servings | **3 cups**   Prep. Time | **10 minutes**   Cook Time | **10 minutes**
**Nut. Content (per serving):** Cal | **326**   Fat | **8.9g**   Protein | **32.4g**   Carbs | **27.9g**

1 1/2 cups spaghetti sauce (homemade or jarred)
1 cup water
1/2 onion (small), diced
1/2 pounds ground lean beef or turkey
1/4 cup parmesan cheese, grated
2 cloves garlic, finely minced or pressed
4 ounces spaghetti noodles, break into thirds
Salt & pepper to taste, adjust as needed

Optional:
1/2 cup bell pepper, chopped
1/2 cup mushrooms, sliced
5 basil leaves (fresh), chopped

1. Set the IP to SAUTE NORMAL mode. Once HOT, add the meat; cook till almost done, occasionally stirring. If using turkey, add a bit of oil in the pot first. Add the onion; cook till they start to turn translucent, occasionally stirring. Add the garlic; stir for a couple of seconds. Add the water and spaghetti sauce; stir to mix.
2. Add the noodles in a crisscross pattern so they are not all lying side by side to prevent them from sticking together. Gently press them under the sauce using a spoon; try to get them all under the liquid, but do not stir.
3. Lock the lid and close the pressure valve. Cancel SAUTÉ. Set the IP to MANUAL HIGH PRESSURE for 9 minutes. NPR for 5 minutes when the timer beeps and QPR; unlock the lid and open.
4. Stir the spaghetti, separating the noodles that are stuck together. Adjust seasoning as needed. Stir in the parmesan. Serve with preferred garnish.

# Game Hen Noodle Soup

Servings | **5 cups**    Prep. Time | **10 minutes**    Cook Time | **11 minutes**
**Nut. Content (per serving):** Cal | **408**    Fat | **23.6g**    Protein | **33.2g**    Carbs | **16.9g**

1 1/2 cups egg noodles (wide)
1 bay leaf
1 celery stalk
1 Cornish rock or game hen
1 onion (small), chopped
1 sprig rosemary (fresh), around 3 to 4-inch long

1 sprig thyme (fresh) or 1/2 teaspoon dried
1/2 teaspoon salt
1/4 teaspoon pepper
2 carrots (medium), chopped
2 teaspoons sage, rubbed
3 cloves garlic, minced or pressed
4 cups water, divided

1. Pour 3 cups water in the IP. Set to SAUTE to start heating up. Slice the hen lengthwise into halves. Put them in the IP with heated water. Lock the lid and close the pressure valve. Cancel SAUTÉ. Set to HIGH PRESSURE for 11 minutes. NPR for 10 minutes when the timer beeps and QPR; unlock the lid and open.

2. Using tongs, transfer the hen to a bowl. Set the IP to SAUTÉ. Stir the soup. Taste and adjust the salt as needed. Add the remaining water in the pot and the noodles; cook for 5 to 8 minutes or till the noodles are cooked.

3. Meanwhile, debone the hen. Shred or break the meat using a fork. Once the noodles are cooked, cancel the SAUTÉ. Add the hen meat into the soup; stir to mix. Serve with crusty bread.

# Meaty Spaghetti

Servings|**2**    Prep. Time|**20 minutes**    Cook Time|**8 minutes**
**Nut. Content (per serving):** Cal|**637**    Fat|**20.5g**    Protein|**53.4g**    Carbs|**58.4g**

1 1/4 cups broth (chicken) or water
1 clove garlic, minced
1 cup spaghetti sauce (jarred)
1 tablespoon olive oil
1/2 pound ground lean beef or turkey
1/2 teaspoon basil (dried)
1/2 teaspoon oregano (dried)

1/2 teaspoon salt
1/2 yellow onion, diced
2 tablespoons Parmesan cheese, with extra to serve
2 tablespoons tomato paste
6 ounces spaghetti noodles
Black pepper (fresh ground)

1. Set the IP to SAUTE. Add the oil and meat; cook for 3 minutes, breaking and stirring using a wooden spoon occasionally. Add the onion; stir for 4 minutes. Add the spaghetti sauce, broth, tomato paste, pepper, salt, oregano, basil, garlic, and parmesan; stir to mix well. Turn the pot off.

2. Break the noodles into halves. Layer them in the mixture, making sure the liquid covers them. Set to HIGH PRESSURE for 8 minutes. Lock the lid and close the pressure valve.

3. QPR very carefully when the timer beeps; unlock the lid and open. The spaghetti may look that it has too much liquid; just stir till it comes together. If there is still too much moisture, set the IP to SAUTÉ; cook for 2 minutes to reduce. You may prefer saucy pasta. Divide between bowls. Top with parmesan and serve.

# Dumplings & Chicken for Two

Servings|**2**     Prep. Time|**25 minutes**     Cook Time|**20 minutes**
**Nut. Content (per serving):** Cal|**901**     Fat|**49.5g**     Protein|**42g**     Carbs|**69.6g**

1 1/2 tablespoons butter (unsalted)
1 carrot (small), diced
1 onion (small), diced
1 quart stock (chicken), preferably homemade
1 stalk celery, diced
1 teaspoon parsley (fresh), minced
1/2 teaspoon salt, more as needed
1/4 teaspoon black pepper (fresh ground)
2 chicken thighs (skin-on & bone-in)
2 tablespoons flour

Dumplings:
1 tablespoon butter, melted
1 teaspoon baking powder
1/2 cup milk
1/2 teaspoon salt
1/4 cup cornmeal (fine)
1/4 teaspoon black pepper (fresh ground)
2 teaspoons parsley (fresh or dried), chopped
3/4 cup flour (all-purpose)

1. Set the IP to SAUTE. Add the butter; let melt and sizzle. With the skin under, add the chicken; sear for 4 to 5 minutes or till golden brown. Flip and sear the other side. Transfer the chicken to a plate.

2. Add the flour to the IP; stir to create a paste. Add the celery, carrot, onion, pepper, salt, and parsley; cook for 2 minutes, stirring occasionally. Add the stock and return the chicken to the pot. Cancel the SAUTE. Set the IP to HIGH PRESSURE for 8 minutes. Lock the lid and close the pressure valve. NPR when the timer beeps; unlock the lid and open. Transfer the chicken to a plate; let cool.

3. Dumplings: Whisk the pepper, salt, parsley, baking powder, cornmeal, and flour to mix well. In another bowl, whisk the milk and butter to mix well. Add the wet ingredients to the dry ingredients; whisk to mix, but do not overmix or you will have tough dumplings.

4. By large tablespoon scoops, drop the dumplings into the IP. Lock the lid and close the pressure valve. Set to HIGH PRESSURE for 2 minutes. QPR when the timer beeps; unlock the lid and open. Shred the chicken meat and divide between bowls. Ladle the dumpling mixture into the bowls. Serve.

# ONE-POT DISHES

## Chicken Biryani

Servings | **6**    Prep. Time | **10 minutes**    Cook Time | **20 minutes**
**Nut. Content (per serving):** Cal | **628**    Fat | **26g**    Protein | **31g**    Carbs | **63g**

Marinade:
1 1/2 pound chicken thighs, boneless &
skinless
1 1/2 teaspoon salt adjust to preference
1 tablespoon coriander powder
1 tablespoon garam masala
1 teaspoon turmeric
1/2 teaspoon chili powder (red) adjust to
preference
2 tablespoons cilantro & mint, chopped
2 tablespoons garlic & ginger paste, 6 cloves
garlic & 1-inch ginger
2 tablespoons olive oil
2 teaspoons cumin powder
2 teaspoons lime juice
2 teaspoons paprika (smoked)
3/4 cup yogurt (plain)

Rice (partial cooking):
1 teaspoon ghee or oil
1/2 teaspoon garam masala
2 cups Rice (Basmati or any long-grain)
2 teaspoons salt
4 cups water

Biryani:
1 tablespoon butter, melted
1 teaspoon garam masala
1/2 cup cilantro & mint, chopped
1/2 teaspoon threads saffron; soak in 2 tbs.
of warm milk
1/4 cup onion (fried)
10 cashews (whole)

Yogurt Dip (mix and refrigerate till serving):
1 cucumber (English), chopped finely
1 tablespoon chopped mint
1/2 teaspoon salt
1/4 teaspoon pepper
1/4 teaspoon sugar, optional, but
recommended
2 cups yogurt (plain)

Fried onions:
3 tablespoons ghee or oil
2 onions, (medium), thinly sliced

1. Fried onion: Set the IP to SAUTE MORE option. Add the ghee and onions. Cook for 12 to 14 minutes, stirring every 3 to 4 minutes till they are golden brown. Transfer and set aside.
2. Chicken: Except for the chicken, mix all the marinade ingredients well. Add the chicken; toss to coat well. Set aside.
3. Rice: Rinse the rice till water runs clear. Soak in warm water for 15 minutes if possible. Strain. Choose preferred partial cooking below.
4. Microwave: Put the rice, garam masala, ghee, and salt in the microwavable bowl; microwave for 10 minutes. Strain and set aside.
5. Stovetop: Boil 4 cups of water in a saucepan. Add the rice, garam masala, ghee, and salt; let come to a boil again. Cook for 5 minutes on high heat. Turn off the heat. Strain the rice and set aside.

6. Biryani: Set the IP to SAUTE. Add 1/4 cup water in the pot if the yogurt used for marinating is thick. Evenly layer the chicken in the pot. Pour the rest of the marinade over them. Layer the partially cooked rice over the chicken. Spread the fried onions on top and the cilantro-mint. Add the cashews and 1 teaspoon garam masala. Add the saffron milk and then the butter.

7. Lock the lid and close the pressure valve. Set to HIGH PRESSURE for 6 minutes. NPR or QPR when the timer beeps; unlock the lid and open. Fluff the rice using a fork. Serve with the yogurt dip.

# Cottage Cheese & Rice with Onion Pickle

Servings|**4**    Prep. Time|**10 minutes**    Cook Time|**10 minutes**
**Nut. Content (per serving):** Cal|**420**    Fat|**18g**    Protein|**14g**    Carbs|**47g**

1 cup & 2 tablespoons water
1 cup rice (Basmati or preferred long-grain), rinsed & soaked for 20 minutes in warm water
1 medium bell pepper (green) sliced
1 onion (medium), sliced
1 teaspoon chaat masala
1 teaspoon cumin powder
1 teaspoon salt
1 teaspoon turmeric powder
1 teaspoon vinegar (red wine) or juice of 1/2 lime
1/2 teaspoon cayenne
10 ounces block paneer (Indian cottage cheese)

2 tablespoons cilantro (fresh), chopped to garnish
2 teaspoons Indian five-spice blend
2 to 3 teaspoon garam masala
2 tomatoes (medium), chopped
3 teaspoons coriander powder

Onion pickle (optional);
1/8 teaspoon cayenne
1/8 teaspoon black pepper
1/4 teaspoon salt
1 teaspoon vinegar (red wine)
1 onion (medium), sliced thin

1. Set the IP to SAUTE. Once HOT, add the oil. Add the five spice blend; sauté for 30 seconds. Add the tomatoes, all the spices, bell pepper, onion, and vinegar; stir and sauté for 1 minute. Add the rice, cheese, and water; stir to mix well. Lock the lid and close the pressure valve. Set to HIGH PRESSURE for 6 minutes. NPR when the timer beeps; unlock the lid and open. Fluff the rice using a fork gently. Garnish with cilantro.
2. Onion pickle: mix all the ingredients till well combined. Refrigerate for 20 minutes. Serve.

# Lamb & Rice

Servings | **4**    Prep. Time | **10 minutes**    Cook Time | **20 minutes**
**Nut. Content (per 1 cup):** Cal | **490**    Fat | **17g**    Protein | **29g**    Carbs | **49g**

1 bell pepper (green), thinly sliced, optional
1 onion, thinly sliced, optional
1 pound boneless leg steak lambs, chunked
into 3/4 to 1-inch cubes

Rice:
1 cup onions (fried)
1 cup extra-long grain rice (Basmati)
1/2 cup cilantro, chopped
1/2 teaspoon saffron
1/2 teaspoon salt adjust to preference
3/4 cup water (warm), adjusted as needed

Marinade
1 tablespoon ghee or oil
1 teaspoon paprika (smoked)
1 teaspoon salt adjust to preference
1/2 cup yogurt (Greek)
1/2 lime juiced
1/2 teaspoon cardamom powder
1/2 teaspoon turmeric powder
1/4 teaspoon cayenne pepper
2 tablespoons garlic & ginger paste, 6 cloves
garlic & 1-inch ginger ground together
3 to 4 teaspoons garam masala

1. Rinse the rice and soak in water for 20 to 30 minutes.
2. Mix all of the marinade ingredients till well combined. Add the peppers, onion, and lamb; mix to coat well. Cover and marinate in the fridge for 20 to 30 minutes or overnight
3. Put the lamb and the marinade in the IP, spreading them in an even layer in the pot. Add the rinsed and drained rise on top of the meat, spreading them evenly. Sprinkle salt over the rice. Distribute the onion (fried) and cilantro on top. Put the saffron in the warm water. Add in the IP. Gently press on the rice so the grains are submerged.
4. Lock the lid and close the pressure valve. Set to HIGH PRESSURE for 6 to 10 minutes. NPR for 10 minutes when the timer beeps and QPR; unlock the lid and open. Gently rice the rice using a fork. Let sit for 5 minutes. Serve warm with yogurt cucumber dip.

# Brown Rice & Kidney Bean Curry

Servings|**4**    Prep. Time|**10 minutes**    Cook Time|**30 minutes**
**Nut. Content (per serving):** Cal|**309**    Fat|**6g**    Protein|**8g**    Carbs|**53g**

Bean Curry:

1 1/2 cups water
1 cup beans (red kidney), soaked overnight
or 1 can
1 onion (small), chopped finely
1 tablespoon garlic & ginger paste, 3 cloves
garlic & 1/2-inch ginger
1 tablespoon olive oil (light) or ghee
1 teaspoon cumin seed
1 teaspoon roasted cumin (ground)

1 teaspoon salt adjust to preference
1 teaspoon turmeric powder
1/4 teaspoon cayenne pepper
2 green chilies, deseeded or whole, optional
2 tablespoons cilantro, chopped, to garnish
2 teaspoons coriander powder
2 teaspoons garam masala
2 tomatoes pureed, or 1 cup crushed

Brown rice:

1 cup & 2 tablespoons water
1 cup brown rice (Basmati or Jasmine),
rinsed

1 teaspoon olive oil (light) or ghee
1/2 teaspoon salt

1. If using dried beans, rinse them and soak in water overnight. Rinse and drain before using. Set the IP to SAUTE MORE mode. After 30 seconds, add the oil, green chilies and cumin seeds. Once the seeds start to splutter, add the onion and garlic & ginger paste; sauté for 30 seconds. Add the crushed tomatoes and all of the spices; sauté for 30 seconds. Add the beans and water; stir to mix.

2. Mix the brown rice, oil, salt, and water in a heatproof bowl. Put the IP trivet on top of the bean mixture. Put the bowl with rice on the trivet. Lock the lid and close the pressure valve. Set to HIGH PRESSURE for 25 minutes. NPR when the timer beeps; unlock the lid and open.

3. Remove the bowl with rice and trivet from the pot. Fluff the rice using a fork. Garnish the bean curry with cilantro. Serve.

## Coconut Lime Chicken & Rice

Servings|**4**   Prep. Time|**10 minutes**   Cook Time|**20 minutes**
**Nut. Content (per serving):** Cal|**195**   Fat|**13g**   Protein|**13g**   Carbs|**5g**

4 to 5 chicken thighs or 2 to 3 Chicken
Breast, fat trimmed, boneless & skinless

Coconut Rice:
1 cup coconut milk
1 cup rice (white long-grain), such as
Jasmine or Basmati
1/4 teaspoon salt

Garnish:
2 tablespoons cilantro, chopped to garnish

Marinade:
1 cup coconut milk, or as needed
1 lime (small) juice & zest
1 tablespoon sugar (brown)
1 tablespoon garlic & ginger chops, or 3
cloves garlic plus 1/2-inch ginger, chopped
1 tablespoon soy sauce (regular or low-sodium)
1 teaspoon cumin (ground)
1/2 teaspoon black pepper (ground)
1/4 teaspoon cayenne pepper, optional
1/4 teaspoon salt, adjust to preference
2 teaspoons coriander powder

1. Mix all of the marinade ingredients in a 1-gallon resealable bag. Score your chicken; add to the bag. Close and toss to coat the chicken well. Marinate in the fridge for 30 minutes up to 2 minutes if possible.
2. Rinse the rice 2 to 3 times or till the water runs clear. If possible, soak for 20 minutes. Mix the rice, water, coconut milk, and salt in a small heatproof pot. Pour the chicken and the marinade in the IP. Set the IP trivet on top of the chicken mixture. Put the pot on the trivet.
3. Lock the lid and close the pressure valve. Set to HIGH PRESSURE for 6 minutes. NPR for 10 minutes when the timer beeps and QPR; unlock the lid and open. Remove the pot and the trivet from the pot. Fluff the rice using a fork. Transfer the chicken to a cutting board; let rest for 5 to 7 minutes before slicing.
4. If desired, set the IP to SAUTÉ; cook for 2 minutes to thicken the sauce. Serve.

# Korean-Spiced Chicken

Servings|**6**    Prep. Time|**5 minutes**    Cook Time|**10 minutes**
**Nut. Content (per serving):** Cal|**353**    Fat|**6g**    Protein|**26g**    Carbs|**46g**

3/4 cup water, or as needed
2 teaspoons olive oil, for cooking
1 1/2 pounds chicken (breasts halves or thighs), boneless & skinless

Marinade:
1 gala apple or pear, blended or grated
1 onion (medium), sliced thin
1 tablespoon garlic paste
1 teaspoon ginger paste
1/2 teaspoon black pepper, crushed
1/4 cup soy sauce
1/4 teaspoon salt, adjust to preference, optional
2 tablespoons chili paste (gochujang Korean)
2 tablespoons vinegar (rice or apple cider)
3 tablespoons honey

Spicy Cucumber Salad:
2 teaspoons sugar adjust to preference
2 teaspoons chili paste (Gochujang Korean), adjust to preference
1/2 teaspoon sesame oil (toasted)
1 teaspoon vinegar (rice or apple cider)
1 teaspoon salt
1 cucumber (English) or 3 to 4 Pickling or Persian cucumbers

Rice:
1/2 teaspoon salt
1 cup water
1 cup jasmine rice (long-grain), rinsed 2 to 3 times or till the water runs clear

Serving suggestion (low-carb):
1 head Butter lettuce for lettuce cups

1. In a mixing bowl (large) or 1-gallon resealable plastic bag, mix all the marinade ingredients together. Add the chicken; mix to coat well. Marinate in the fridge for 1 hour.
2. Set the IP to SAUTE. Add the oil. Once heated, add the chicken and the marinade. Add a very small amount of water because the chicken will release moisture as it cooks. Put the IP trivet on top of the chicken mixture. In a heatproof bowl, mix the rice, salt, and water; set on the trivet.
3. Lock the lid and close the pressure valve. Set to HIGH PRESSURE for 6 minutes. NPR for 10 minutes when the timer beeps and QPR; unlock the lid and open.
4. Transfer the chicken to a slicing board and slice if desired. To thicken the sauce, set the IP to SAUTÉ. Cook for 2 to 3 minutes or till thick. Return the chicken in the pot. Mix to coat with the sauce.

# Butter Chicken & Saffron Rice

Servings|4    Prep. Time|**5 minutes**    Cook Time|**20 minutes**
**Nut. Content (per serving):** Cal|**371**    Fat|**22g**    Protein|**34g**    Carbs|**7g**

Butter chicken:
1 1/2 pounds chicken (breasts or thighs), boneless & skinless, sliced into in 3-inch pieces
1 tablespoon olive oil (light) or oil (vegetable)
2 tablespoons garlic & ginger paste, 1-inch ginger & 6 cloves garlic, grated or pulsed
14 ounces (canned) diced tomatoes, pureed, OR 3 to4 tomatoes (ripe Roma), pureed
1 teaspoon salt
1/2 teaspoon Turmeric Powder
1/4 to 1/2 teaspoon Chili powder (red)
2 teaspoons Paprika (smoked)
2 to 3 teaspoons Garam Masala adjust to preference
1 tablespoon Coriander Powder

After cooking:
1/2 cup cream (heavy whipping) or Coconut milk (full fat)
1 to 2 teaspoons sugar optional
2 to 3 tablespoons cilantro (fresh), chopped

Saffron rice:
1 cup rice (Basmati or Jasmine)
1 cup water
1 teaspoon ghee or oil
1/2 teaspoon saffron, soaked in 1 tablespoon hot water or microwaved with the water for 20 to 30 seconds
1/2 teaspoon salt
2 tablespoons almonds (slivered), optional

1. Rice: Rinse the rice 2 to 3 times or till the water runs clear. If possible, soak them in water for 15 minutes and drain. Put the saffron in a microwavable bowl, break them down into small pieces. Add 1 tablespoon hot water. Or add cold water and microwave for 20 to 30 seconds.  Put the rice, saffron, salt, oil, almonds, and water in a heatproof bowl; set aside.
2. Sauce: Set the IP to SAUTE.  Add the oil, tomato sauce, spices, garlic & ginger paste, and chicken; stir to mix well. Set the IP trivet on top of the meat mixture. Place the bowl with rice on the trivet. Lock the lid and close the pressure valve. Set to HIGH PRESSURE for 6 minutes. NPR for 10 minutes when the timer beeps and QPR; unlock the lid and open.
3. Remove the bowl with rice from the pot carefully; fluff using a fork and set aside. Set the IP to SAUTE. Add the cream or coconut milk; sauté for 2 to 3 minutes or till slightly thickened. Add the optional sugar and mix. Serve garnished with cilantro and with a side of naan and saffron rice.

## Thai Chicken & Veggie Curry

Servings|**4**    Prep. Time|**10 minutes**    Cook Time|**20 minutes**
**Nut. Content (per serving):** Cal|**591**    Fat|**32g**    Protein|**43g**    Carbs|**35g**

1 1/2 pounds chicken (thighs or breasts), skinless & boneless, chunked to bite-sized pieces
1 cup carrot chunks
1 onion (small), sliced or cubed
1 tablespoon olive oil (light)
1/2-inch ginger pureed or grated
14 ounces baby corn (canned), sliced
14 ounces coconut milk (canned)

2 cloves garlic pureed or grated
4 ounces curry (canned), Maesri Thai Masaman

After cooking:
1 cup broccoli florets
1 cup beans (French), sliced to bite-sized pieces

1. Set the IP to SAUTE. Add the oil. Once heated, add the chicken, ginger, garlic, and curry paste; sauté for 30 to 45 seconds. Add the corn, onion, carrot, and coconut milk; stir to mix well. Let come to a simmer and bubbly to prevent the coconut milk from curdling.
2. Lock the lid and close the pressure valve. Set to HIGH PRESSURE for 5 minutes. NPR for 10 minutes when the timer beeps and QPR; unlock the lid and open.
3. Set the IP to SAUTE. Add the beans; cook for 2 to 3 minutes. Cancel SAUTE. Add the broccoli; let cook for 2 to 3 minutes with the residual heat. Squeeze a few drops of lime juice to finish.

## Rice & Jerk Thighs

Servings|**2**    Prep. Time|**10 minutes**    Cook Time|**8 minutes**
**Nut. Content (per serving):** Cal|**0**    Fat|**0g**    Protein|**0g**    Carbs|**0g**

1 clove garlic, finely minced or pressed
1 cup broth (chicken) (low-sodium)
1 tablespoon Jamaican jerk seasoning
1/2 sweet onion (small), diced

2 chicken thighs (frozen or fresh), boneless & skinless
2 teaspoon olive oil
3/4 cup white rice (long-grain), rinsed very well & drained

1. Prepare the rice. Set the IP to SAUTE NORMAL mode. Once, HOT, add the oil. Add the onion; stir and cook for a couple of minutes till starting to turn translucent. Add the garlic; stir for 20 seconds. Add the seasoning; stir well. Stir in the broth; let come to a simmer. Stir in the rice, making sure every grain is submerged. Lay the chicken on top of the mixture, submerging them if possible.
2. Lock the lid and close the pressure valve. Cancel SAUTE. Set to MANUAL HIGH PRESSURE for 7 minutes. NPR for 5 minutes when the timer beeps and QPR; unlock the lid and open. Remove the chicken from the pot. You can either serve the rice with 1 thigh each or shred the meat and then mix it with the rice.
NOTES: You can use taco or Cajun seasoning for a different flavor.

# Bulgogi or Korean Beef

Servings | **4-6**   Prep. Time | **20 minutes**   Cook Time | **12 minutes**
**Nut. Content (per serving):** Cal | **514**   Fat | **15.1g**   Protein | **39.1g**   Carbs | **53.6g**

1 1/2 pounds ground beef, preferably 90% lean
1 tablespoon grated ginger root or 1 teaspoon ginger powder
1 tablespoon sesame oil
1/2 pear (Asian), grated, optional
1/2 teaspoon white or black pepper
1/3 cup sugar (brown)
1/3 cup soy sauce (low-sodium)
1/3 cup water
2 teaspoons oil (vegetable)
3/4 teaspoon flakes red pepper, or more as desired
7 cloves (1 tablespoon) pressed garlic

Rice:
7 x 2 1/2-inch pan
1 1/2 cups rice (Jasmine), rinsed
1 1/2 cups water
2 tablespoons butter

To serve:
Lettuce leaves (for lettuce wraps)
Tortillas (for tacos)

Garnish:
2 green onions, sliced
Sesame seeds

1. Before cooking, prepare all the ingredients. Ready the rice pan to go as needed.
2. Set the IP to SAUTE. Once HOT, add the oil and beef; cook till the meat is no longer pink. Drain excess fat as needed, leaving only a couple teaspoons in the pot. Add the water, pepper, red pepper, pear, ginger, sesame oil, sugar, and soy sauce; mix well. Cancel the SAUTE.
3. Set an IP trivet on top to the beef mixture. Put the pan with the rice, water, and butter mixture on the trivet. Lock the lid and close the pressure valve. Set to MANUAL HIGH PRESSURE for 4 minutes. NPR for 9 minutes when the timer beeps and QPR; unlock the lid and open.
4. Remove the pan with rice from the pot; fluff the rice using a fork. Remove the trivet; stir the beef mixture. Serve the bulgogi over the rice, in tacos or tortillas, or lettuce leaves. Garnish and serve.

# Salsa Chicken

Servings | **4**    Prep. Time | **25 minutes**    Cook Time | **10 minutes**
**Nut. Content (per serving):** Cal | **484**    Fat | **17.9g**    Protein | **32g**    Carbs | **48.5g**

1 clove garlic, minced
1 cup stock (chicken)
1 cup white rice (long-grain), rinsed
1 onion (small), diced
1 tablespoon olive oil
1/2 teaspoon coriander (ground)
1/2 teaspoon cumin

1/4 teaspoon salt
16 ounces salsa
2 chicken breasts (boneless, skinless w/ rib meat)
4 ounces Mexican blend cheese
Black pepper (fresh ground)
Cilantro, to serve

1. Set the IP to SAUTE. Add the oil and onion; cook for 4 minutes or till the onions are translucent. Add your garlic; fry for around 15 seconds. Turn off the pot.
2. Add the rice, pepper, salt, coriander, cumin, salsa, and stock; stir to mix very well. Lay the chicken on top. Set the IP to HIGH PRESSURE for 10 minutes. Lock the lid and close the pressure valve. NPR for 10 minutes when the timer beeps and QPR; unlock the lid and open.
3. Fluff the rice using a fork. Transfer the mixture to a bowl. While still hot, add the cheese, stir to mix. Shred the chicken or leave them whole. Garnish with cilantro; serve. Top with more cheese, cilantro, or olives. You can roll the mixture in tortilla, drizzle with enchilada sauce, and bake. You can top with fried eggs for a delicious brunch. Keep leftovers stored covered in the fridge.

# STOCKS, SAUCES, DIPS, & SPREADS

## Homemade Hummus

Servings | **4**    Prep. Time | **5 minutes**    Cook Time | **50 minutes**
**Nut. Content (per serving):** Cal | **542**    Fat | **26.3g**    Protein | **19.5g**    Carbs | **61.6g**

1 tablespoon oil (vegetable)
1 teaspoon salt
1/2 teaspoon pepper
1/3 cup olive oil, divided, with extra to serve

2 cups chickpeas aka garbanzo beans (dried)
3 garlic cloves, peeled & smashed
Pita bread, cucumbers, carrots, and peppers, to serve

1. Put the garlic and beans in the IP. Add 5 cups of water; stir to mix. Add the oil. Lock the lid and close the pressure valve. Set to BEAN/CHILI for 50 minutes. NPR for 10 minutes when the timer beeps and QPR; unlock the lid and open.
2. Set a colander on a bowl (large) in your sink. Pour the chickpeas in the colander to drain and the bowl to catch the cooking liquid; save the liquid for later.
3. Transfer the beans in your food processor. Add 1/4 cup of the cooking liquid, 3 tablespoons oil, pepper, and salt. Pulse till blended. Increase the power to HIGH; gradually add the rest of the oil and more of the reserved cooking liquid as needed till the mixture is smooth.
4. Transfer to a serving bowl. Drizzle with 1 tablespoon oil more; season with black pepper (freshly cracked). Serve with pita bread, cucumbers, carrots, and peppers.

## Hot Sauce

Servings | **0**    Prep. Time | **5 minutes**    Cook Time | **6 minutes**
**Nut. Content (per 1 tbsp.)** Cal | **7**    Fat | **0g**    Protein | **0g**    Carbs | **1.3g**

1 1/4 cup (300 milliliters) vinegar (apple cider) ore preferred kind, less or more as needed

12 ounces (350 grams) hot peppers (fresh, any kind), stems removed
2 teaspoons salt (smoked or plain)

1. Roughly chop the hot peppers. Put them in the IP. Add just enough vinegar to cover them. Add the salt. Lock the lid and close the pressure valve. Set to HIGH PRESSURE for 1 minute. Cancel the KEEP WARM mode and unplug when the timer beeps. NPR for 10 to 15 minutes or till the indicator is down and QPR; unlock the lid and open.
2. Puree using an immersion blender and then strain into a freshly cleaned or sterilized bottle. Keep refrigerated for 3 months or store in freezable containers to freeze for up to 1 year.

## Creamy Basil-Tomato Pasta Sauce

Servings | **1 pound**     Prep. Time | **5 minutes**     Cook Time | **5 minutes**
**Nut. Content (per 1/4 pound):** Cal | **104**     Fat | **4.5g**     Protein | **4.4g**     Carbs | **13.3g**

1 tablespoon tomato paste
1/2 cup cream (heavy)
1/2 cup evaporated milk (low-fat or regular)
1/2 tablespoon leaves rosemary (fresh) chopped, optional
1/4 teaspoon salt (table)

1/4 yellow onion (small) chopped (1/4 cup)
1/8 loosely packed cup basil leaves (fresh) roughly chopped
28 ounces (canned) whole tomatoes, drained

1. Wash your hands and dry them. Individually crush the tomatoes into the pot. Add the salt, rosemary, basil, onion, and milk; stir to mix well. Lock the lid and close the pressure valve. Set to HIGH PRESSURE for 5 minutes. QPR when the timer beeps; unlock the lid and open.
2. Stir in the tomato paste and cream. Puree using an immersion blender right in the pot or transfer to a regular blender to puree till smooth.

## Sweet & Spicy Lemon Pickle

Servings | **12**     Prep. Time | **0 minutes**     Cook Time | **30 minutes**
**Nut. Content (per serving):** Cal | **37**     Fat | **1g**     Protein | **0g**     Carbs | **6g**

6 lemons (medium)

Roasting spice mixture:
1 teaspoon fennel seeds
1 teaspoon fenugreek seeds
1 teaspoon mustard seeds (black)

For tempering:
1 tablespoon olive oil
1 teaspoon chili powder (Kashmiri red), or
1/4 to 1/2 teaspoon cayenne
1 teaspoon salt
1/2 teaspoon mustard seeds
6 tablespoons sugar (brown)

1. Wash the lemons and then dry them. Put the IP trivet in the inner pot and pour 1 cup water. Put the lemons on a bowl and set the bowl on the trivet. Lock the lid and close the pressure valve. Set to HIGH PRESSURE for 15 minutes.
2. Meanwhile, put the roasting spice ingredients in a microwavable plate; microwave in 30-second intervals for 3 minutes, stirring between. Let cool for 5 minutes; grind into a fine powder using a spice blender.
3. NPR when the timer beeps; unlock the lid and open. Remove the lemons, slice them into halves, and remove the seeds. Set the IP to SAUTÉ; let heat for 30 seconds. Add the oil and mustard seeds. Once they start sizzling, add the lemons, sugar, and spices; stir to mix well.
4. Sauté for 4 to 5 minutes or till the liquid is jam-like. Turn OFF the IP. For the best result, let rest for 4 to 5 days in the fridge before consuming.

## Instant Clarified Butter or Ghee

Servings|**28**    Prep. Time|**5 minutes**    Cook Time|**20 minutes**
**Nut. Content (per 1 tbsp.):** Cal|**116**    Fat|**13g**    Protein|**0g**    Carbs|**0g**

16 ounces butter (unsalted)

1. Set the IP to SAUTE NORMAL mode. Switch to LESS mode if your pot tends to heat faster. Add the butter in the pot; set an external timer for 7 minutes. Keep an eye on the butter at the end of the 7 minutes. The butter will turn to ghee in around 12 to 13 minutes.
2. The ghee is done when it is clear and you can see the bottom of the pot. The milk that will solidify at the bottom of the pot will be caramelized and grainier (golden) brownish, which is fine. Turn OFF the IP. Let cool for 5 to 10 minutes. Carefully remove the inner pot from the housing to prevent the ghee from cooking further.
3. Strain the ghee using a fine sieve or cheesecloth into dry, clean storage bottles. Store in the fridge or a dark, cool place. It will stay good for 1 month bring to temperature and for 6 months in the fridge.

## Master Curry Sauce

Servings|**6**    Prep. Time|**10 minutes**    Cook Time|**10 minutes**
**Nut. Content (per serving):** Cal|**44**    Fat|**2g**    Protein|**0g**    Carbs|**4g**

1 onion (medium), chopped finely
1 tablespoon ghee or olive oil
1 teaspoon cumin seeds
1 teaspoon paprika or paprika (smoked), optional
1 teaspoon roasted cumin (ground)
1 teaspoon salt
1 to 2 teaspoons garam masala, adjust to preference

1/2 cup water
1/2 teaspoon cayenne pepper adjust to preference
1/2 teaspoon turmeric powder
1-inch ginger, peeled & chopped finely
2 teaspoons coriander powder
2 tomatoes (plum) pureed, or 1 cup crushed tomatoes
6 cloves garlic, peeled & chopped finely

1. Set the IP to SAUTE. Add the oil. Once heated for 30 seconds, add the cumin seeds. When they start to splutter, add the ginger, onion, and garlic; sauté for 1 to 2 minutes or till golden brown.
2. Add the tomatoes; scrape the brown bits off the pot with a wooden spoon. Add the water and spices; stir well. Press CANCEL. Lock the lid and close the pressure valve. Set to HIGH PRESSURE for 5 minutes. NPR for 10 minutes when the timer beeps and QPR; unlock the lid and open.

## Pigeon Peas Dip

Servings|**4**   Prep. Time|**5 minutes**   Cook Time|**25 minutes**
**Nut. Content (per serving):** Cal|**64**   Fat|**0g**   Protein|**3g**   Carbs|**12g**

Peas:
1 1/2 cups water, or as needed, enough to cover the peas
1 cup pigeon peas (whole)
1 teaspoon salt
1/2 inch ginger, grated, or 1/2 teaspoon ginger powder
1/2 teaspoon cayenne powder
2 teaspoons coriander powder

Dressing:
1 teaspoon Chaat Masala
1 teaspoon cumin powder (roasted)
1/2 lime juiced, adjust to preference
1/4 cup (around 1 Roma) tomato, deseeded & chopped finely
1/4 cup cilantro, chopped
1/4 cup onion (around 1/4 large), chopped finely

1. Rinse the peas for 2 to 3 times. Soak with 3 cups water for 6 to 8 hours or overnight. Rinse and drain before using. Add to the IP with fresh water enough to cover them. Lock the lid and close the pressure valve. Set to BEAN for 15 minutes. NPR for 10 minutes when the timer beeps and QPR; unlock the lid and open. Let cool for 10 minutes.
2. Add the seasonings, cilantro, tomatoes, and onions; gently stir to mix. Serve with cucumber slices or pita chips as an appetizer or serve with sourdough bread (toasted) or naan for a filling meal.

## Roasted Garlic

Servings|**0**   Prep. Time|**0 minutes**   Cook Time|**15 minutes**
**Nut. Content (per serving):** Cal|**0**   Fat|**0g**   Protein|**0g**   Carbs|**0g**

1 cup water
3 garlic bulbs (large)

Drizzle olive oil (extra-virgin), use the good kind

1. Put the IP steamer basket in the inner pot and pour 1 cup water. Slice the 1/4 top of the garlic bulbs; save the garlic tips that will easily pop out of the cut tops for other recipes. Put the bulbs in the basket.
2. Lock the lid and close the pressure valve. Set to HIGH PRESSURE for 6 minutes. Cancel the KEEP WARM mode and unplug when the timer beeps. NPR for 10 to 15 minutes or till the indicator is down and QPR; unlock the lid and open.
3. Using tongs, carefully remove the soft, hot garlic from the pot and transfer to a heatproof dish. Drizzle all the nooks and crannies with the olive oil. Broil for 5 minutes or till caramelized and golden. Serve.

# Super Healthy, Delicious, Chunky Pasta Sauce

Servings | **2**　　Prep. Time | **5 minutes**　　Cook Time | **10 minutes**
**Nut. Content (per serving):** Cal | **640**　　Fat | **30g**　　Protein | **54g**　　Carbs | **46g**

1 onion (small), sliced into chunks
1 pound ground beef, chicken, or turkey (or a mixture
1 tablespoon olive oil (extra-virgin)
1 teaspoon salt, adjust to preference
1/2 teaspoon black pepper, adjust to preference
1/2 teaspoon red pepper (crushed), adjust to preference
2 carrots (medium), sliced into chunks
2 cups cremini mushrooms
28 ounces Marinara sauce or crushed tomatoes
3 garlic cloves

4 teaspoons Italian seasoning, use 2 teaspoons only if using marinara sauce
Meat (omit for a vegetarian sauce)
Preferred veggies for blending (anything you have to make 2 1/2 to 3 cups chopped)

Cheese:
1/4 cup parmesan cheese or similar blend, grated

Garnish:
1/4 cup parsley, chopped
2 tablespoons basil (fresh), hand torn

1. Put the garlic in your food processor; pulse for 5 to 6 times or till finely chopped. Add the carrots; repeat the process till finely chopped. Add the mushrooms; pulse 5 to 7 times till finely chopped. Transfer the mixture to a bowl.
2. Put the onion in the food processor; pulse for 5 to 6 times or till finely chopped. Add to the bowl with chopped veggies.
3. Set the IP to SAUTE MORE mode. Add the olive oil. Once HOT, add the meat; do not stir for 1 minute or so or till the underside is brown. Skip this step if making vegetarian. Break the meat using a spatula or wooden spoon; stir to mix. Add the chopped veggies; sauté for 1 minute. Add the crushed tomatoes, marinara, and spices; stir to mix well. If the sauce looks too thick, add 1/2 to 1/4 cup of water.
4. Lock the lid and close the pressure valve. Set to HIGH PRESSURE for 3 to 4 minutes. NPR for 5 to 7 minutes when the timer beeps and QPR; unlock the lid and open. Stir in the cheese. Garnish with parsley or basil just before serving.

## Potato-Cauliflower Garlic Sauce

Servings|**6**    Prep. Time|**10 minutes**    Cook Time|**20 minutes**
**Nut. Content (per serving):** Cal|**141**    Fat|**10g**    Protein|**3g**    Carbs|**9g**

Steam:
6 cloves garlic adjust to preference, peeled
2 potatoes (large gold), peeled & quartered
(around 1 1/2 cups)
1/2 head cauliflower (around 2 cups) florets
only, rinsed & drained

After making the sauce:
2 to 3 tablespoons parmesan cheese
(grated)

After cooking:
1 1/2 tablespoon goat cheese, bring to
room temperature
1 tablespoon butter (unsalted) bring to
room temperature
1/2 cup cream (heavy whipping) or half-&-
half (adjust to preference)
1/2 teaspoon salt, adjust to preference
1/4 teaspoon black pepper (ground), adjust
to preference

1. Put the IP steamer basket in the inner pot and pour 1 cup water. Put the garlic, potatoes, and cauliflower in the basket. Lock the lid and close the pressure valve. Set to HIGH PRESSURE for 8 minutes. QPR when the timer beeps; unlock the lid and open. Transfer the veggies to mixing bowl (large).
2. Heat the cream (heavy) in a microwavable cup for 2 minutes in the microwave. Add the pepper, salt, cheese, and butter; whisk well till smooth. Pour over the steamed veggies. Mash the mixture using a wooden spoon or fork till creamy. Add the cheese; whisk till well mixed. Serve with chicken or lamb chops.

## Cranberry Sauce

Servings|**1 cup**    Prep. Time|**1 minute** Cook Time|**14 minutes**
**Nut. Content (per 3 tsp.):** Cal|**30.1**    Fat|**0.1g**    Protein|**0g**    Carbs|**7.9g**

1 cup (140 grams) cranberries (dried)
1 teaspoon lemon juice

3/4 cup (180 milliliters) cranberry juice
cocktail
3/4 cup (180 milliliters) water

1. Put all the ingredients in the IP. Lock the lid and close the pressure valve. Set to HIGH PRESSURE for 3 minutes. QPR gradually when the timer beeps; unlock the lid and open.
2. With an immersion blender, partially puree the mixture using a couple of quick pulses, tilting the pot to keep the blender immersed. Just break a couple of the berries, do not liquefy.
3. Set the IP to SAUTE. Let come to a simmer; cook for 5 minutes or till desired thickness is achieved. Once you can drag a spatula or spoon across the base of your IP and reveal the bottom, turn of the pot. Let stand uncovered for 10 minutes. Serve warm or transfer to a container with tight lid and keep refrigerated for 1 week. The sauce will thicken more as it cools.

# Ragu Bolognese Pasta Sauce

Servings | **6-8**     Prep. Time | **10 minutes**     Cook Time | **1 hour**
**Nut. Content (per serving):** Cal | **209.3**     Fat | **14.8g**     Protein | **9.5g**     Carbs | **6.7g**

1 carrot (medium), chopped
1 celery stalk (medium), chopped
1 cup (250milliliters) stock (beef)
1 onion (medium), chopped
1 tablespoon cream (heavy)
1 teaspoon salt
1 to 1 1/2 cups water, (hot)

1/2 cup (125 milliliters) wine (dry red), such as Sangiovese
1/4 teaspoon pepper
11 ounces (300 grams) beef, ground
4 ounces (100 grams) pancetta, or unsmoked bacon, cubed
5 tablespoons tomato paste concentrate

1. Lay the pancetta flat in the IP. Set the IP to SAUTE LESS mode. Once sizzling and the fat renders, add the celery, carrot, and onion. Set the pot to SAUTE NORMAL mode; cook for 10 minutes or till the veggies are soft. Add a bit of olive oil or butter if the ingredients start sticking.
2. Add the beef; cook for 30 minutes or till brown, the fat sizzles, and the meat juices have evaporated, occasionally stirring. Add the wine; scrape the brown bits off the pot. Cook for 7 minutes or till the wine has completely evaporated. Meanwhile, mix the stock, tomato paste, pepper, and salt. Pour the mixture in the pot; stir to mix well.
3. Lock the lid and close the pressure valve. Set to HIGH PRESSURE for 10 minutes. QPR when the timer beeps; unlock the lid and open. Add 1 1/2 cups hot water; stir to mix and scrape the juicy bits off the pot.
4. Lock the lid and close the pressure valve. Set to HIGH PRESSURE for 10 minutes. QPR when the timer beeps; unlock the lid and open. Stir in the cream to mix well. Serve.
NOTES: This sauce is good for 500 grams or 16 ounces of pasta or 1 large lasagna.

# Chickpea Hummus

Servings|**6-8**    Prep. Time|**5 minutes**    Cook Time|**25 minutes**
**Nut. Content (per 8 servings):** Cal|**109.1**    Fat|**3.8g**    Protein|**4.1g**    Carbs|**3.3g**

1 bay leaf, crumbled
1 cup (180 grams) chickpeas (dry), quick-soaked or soaked overnight
1 garlic clove
1 lemon, juiced (around 3 tablespoons juice)
Pinch paprika

1 sprig parsley, chopped finely
1/2 teaspoon salt (sea), adjust to preference
1/4 teaspoon cumin (powdered)
2 heaping tablespoons tahini
4 cups (1 liter) water
Olive oil (extra-virgin)

1. Rinse the chickpeas. Put them in the IP. Add enough water to cover them. Add the bay leaf. Lock the lid and close the pressure valve. Set to HIGH PRESSURE for 18 minutes. NPR for 10 minutes when the timer beeps and QPR; unlock the lid and open.
2. Drain the chickpeas; save the cooking liquid. You will use some to puree the chickpeas. Use the rest as stock in your risotto. Reserve some whole chickpeas as garnish if desired.
3. Let the drained chickpeas cool for 30 minutes. Remove the bay leaf. Transfer the cooled chickpeas in your food processor or use an immersion blender or potato masher. Add around 1/2 cup of the cooking juices in the puree. Add the garlic, cumin, lemon juice, and tahini. Puree till smooth. Gradually add cooking juices till desired consistency is achieved. When the texture is right add the salt and puree again to mix well. Transfer to a large dipping bowl or to individual serving bowls. Create a well in the center; add a generous amount of your best olive oil in the well. Season with paprika and garnish with parsley, along with the reserved whole cooked chickpeas. Serve.

## Pancetta & Artichoke Egg Pasta Sauce

Servings|**8**　Prep. Time|**10 minutes**　Cook Time|**15 minutes**
**Nut. Content (per serving):** Cal|**222**　Fat|**11.6g**　Protein|**15.5g**　Carbs|**14.7g**

1 garlic clove, smashed
1 lemon
1/2 cup cheese (Pecorino Romano), grated
1/2 cup wine (white)
2 sprigs parsley, chopped

3 1/2 ounces (100 grams) pancetta or bacon, diced
4 fresh eggs (top-quality)
6 artichokes, cleaned and sliced
Black pepper, fresh ground

1. Mix the juice of 1 to 2 lemons and water in a bowl (large). Remove the outer leaves and peel the outer skin of each artichoke. Slice the 1/3 top of the leaves off. Slice each piece lengthwise into halves. With a melon baller, scoop the hearts out. Slice the clean halves into small wedges. Quickly toss them in the prepared lemon juice mixture to prevent them from oxidizing.
2. Put the pancetta in the IP; set to SAUTE LESS mode. When they start to sizzle and the fat renders, around 5 minutes, add the garlic. Once the pancetta is golden, remove them from the pot; set aside.
3. Set the IP to SAUTE NORMAL mode, strain the artichokes and add in the pot. Stir to coat with the pancetta fat; cook for 5 minutes or till the artichokes are slightly golden. Add the wine to deglaze the pot. Scrape the brown bits off the pot using a spatula and mix.
4. Lock the lid and close the pressure valve. Set to HIGH PRESSURE for 5 to 7 minutes. QPR when the timer beeps; unlock the lid and open. While the pot is depressurizing, mix the cheese, eggs, and pepper in a bowl.
5. Cook your pasta according to package instructions. You can cook 1 pound or 500 grams of preferred pasta for this sauce. When your pasta is almost al dente. Ladle some of the pasta cooking water to the bowl with the egg mixture, stirring as your pour to temper the eggs. Strain the pasta and return to the pan. Immediately pour the egg mixture over the pasta while stirring. Stir in the artichokes, pancetta, and the parsley. Serve!

# Delicious 7-Layer Veggie Dip

Servings|6    Prep. Time|**30minutes**    Cook Time|**15 minutes**
**Nut. Content (per serving):** Cal|**213**    Fat|**16.8g**    Protein|**7.8**    Carbs|**18.7g**

Refried bean:
1 cup kidney beans (dried), soaked overnight, rinsed, & strained
1 cup water
1 onion (small), roughly chopped
1 tablespoon olive oil
1 teaspoon salt
1/2 small Ancho chili (dried), stem removed, or 1/4 teaspoon flakes hot pepper)
3/4 teaspoon cumin powder

Cheese:
1 cup cheddar cheese, grated

Remaining Layers:
1 green onion, sliced finely into rounds
1/4 cup black olives, sliced

Guacamole:
Pinch salt
1 teaspoon lemon or lime juice
1 garlic clove, crushed
1 avocado (large), mashed

Cream:
1 cup (250 milliliters) milk yogurt (plain whole), usually sour cream

Salsa:
3 sprigs parsley or cilantro, chopped finely
1/8 onion (small), chopped finely
1 tomato (large), diced small & strained

1. Beans: Set the IP to SAUTE. Once HOT, add the oil and onion; sauté for 5 minutes or till the onion is soft. Add the cumin powder and chili; sauté for 1 minute. Add the beans and water.
2. Lock the lid and close the pressure valve. Set to HIGH PRESSURE for 8 minutes. Cancel the KEEP WARM mode and unplug when the timer beeps. NPR for 10 to 15 minutes or till the indicator is down and QPR; unlock the lid and open. While the beans are pressure cooking and cooling, prepare the layers.
3. Open the IP. Add the salt. Puree the mixture using an immersion blender, tilting the pan to immerse the blender completely. Cover the pot with the lid to keep warm till ready to use.
4. Layer the ingredients: Grate your cheese. Mix the ingredients for your guacamole. Remove any liquid from the top of your yogurt. Mix your ingredients for the tomato salsa; put it in a strainer (fine mesh), and let excess liquid drain. Pull out the green onions and black olives.
5. Layer the ingredients: In individual glasses or a bowl (large), layer the ingredients by spooning them in the middle then spread them to the edges, like frosting a cake. Layer the beans, cheese, and guacamole. When you reach the yogurt layer, completely spread them over the guacamole layer to seal it tightly and prevent it from turning black. Pile the salsa on top of the yogurt layer. Sprinkle with olives and green onion on to. Serve with corn chips, baked tortilla chips, or your preferred veggie dipping.
https://www.hippressurecooking.com/fresh-make-the-7-layer-dip-from-scratch/

# Mango Chutney

Servings | **48**     Prep. Time | **5 minutes**     Cook Time | **20 minutes**
**Nut. Content (per 1 tablespoon.):** Cal | **78.2**     Fat | **0.3g**     Protein | **0.9g**     Carbs | **18.3g**

1 1/4 cups vinegar (apple cider) or 1 cup vinegar (wine white)
1 apple, skin-on, cored & diced
1 shallot, chopped
1 tablespoon oil (vegetable)
1/4 cup raisins
1/4 teaspoon cardamom powder

1/8 teaspoon cinnamon
11/4 cups sugar (raw demerara)
2 fresh chili (red hot), chopped finely or 1/2 teaspoon flakes red pepper
2 large mangoes, diced
2 tablespoons ginger (fresh), finely diced
2 teaspoons salt

1. Set the IP to SAUTE. Once HOT, add the oil, ginger, and shallots; sauté till the shallots start to soften. Add the hot peppers, cinnamon, and cardamom; sauté for 1 minute or till the spices are fragrant. Add the rest of the ingredients; stir to mix well and the sugar completely dissolves.
2. Lock the lid and close the pressure valve. Set to HIGH PRESSURE for 5 to 7 minutes. Cancel the KEEP WARM mode and unplug when the timer beeps. NPR for 10 to 15 minutes or till the indicator is down and QPR; unlock the lid and open.
3. Set the IP to SAUTE NORMAL mode; let come to a simmer. Cook for about 15 minutes or till you can see the bottom when you drag a spatula or spoon across the bottom of the pot. Stir occasionally at the beginning. As the mixture thickens, set the IP to KEEP WARM mode and stir frequently.
4. Scoop the piping hot chutney to clean jars; tightly close. Once cool, refrigerate for up to 1 month. You can transfer to freezable containers and freeze for up to 1 year.

# Ricotta

Servings|**8 ounces**    Prep. Time|**1 minute** Cook Time|**30 minutes**
**Nut. Content (per 1/4 cup):** Cal|**108**    Fat|**8g**    Protein|**7g**    Carbs|**2g**

1 lemon, squeezed (around 4 tablespoons juice)

1 quart (1 liter) whole milk (high quality)
2 pinch salt, optional

1. Put the milk in the IP. Lock the lid and set pressure valve to VENT. Set to YOGURT and adjust to BOIL. When the program is completed after 20 to 30 minutes, remove the insert from the housing and set on a trivet on the counter.
2. Pour 1/2 of the lemon juice in the pot; delicately and slowly stir – the milk will start to coagulate. If nothing happens after 2 minutes, add the rest of the juice; continue stirring slowly.
3. Pour the mixture through a strainer (fine mesh) or a regular strainer lined with a coffee filter, paper towel (unbleached), or fine cheesecloth. Sprinkle with salt. Let drain for 5 to 15 minutes or till only the milk solids remain.
4. With a spoon or spatula, push the outer edges of the ricotta towards the center to create a small, round piece, lightly squeezing and pressing. Flip it onto a serving dish (small) or a refrigerator container (plastic) and keep refrigerated for 5 days.
5. Save the strained liquid for other use, such as stock for rice or water for baking projects.

# Small Batch Chicken Stock

Servings|**1 quart**    Prep. Time|**15 minutes**    Cook Time|**30 minutes**
**Nut. Content (per 1 cup):** Cal|**10**    Fat|**0.6g**    Protein|**0.7g**    Carbs|**0.7g**

1 bay leaf
1 carrot (large)
1 onion (small), washed well & chopped into half

1 teaspoon salt
2 celery stalks
2 chicken thighs (skin-on & bone-in)
2 peppercorns

1. Except for the salt, put the rest of the ingredients in the IP. Add enough water to reach the maximum fill line. Lock the lid and close the pressure valve. Set to MANUAL HIGH PRESSURE for 30 minutes. NPR or QPR when the timer beeps; unlock the lid and open.
2. Strain the mixture into a bowl with a spout; discard the solids. Stir the salt in the broth till completely dissolved. Transfer the broth into a mason jar (1-quart); keep refrigerated for up to 5 days or store in freezer bags and freeze for months.

# BBQ Sauce

Servings | **2 1/2 cups**    Prep. Time | **5 minutes**    Cook Time | **15 minutes**
**Nut. Content (per 1 tablespoon.):** Cal | **20.3**    Fat | **0.4g**    Protein | **0.1g**    Carbs | **4.5g**

1 onion (medium), roughly chopped
1 tablespoon sesame seed ore preferred
high-smoking point oil, such as grapeseed
oil, peanut, or avocado
1 teaspoon hot sauce
1 teaspoon liquid smoke
1 teaspoon salt (sea)
1/2 cup (120milliliters) tomato puree or
passata
1/2 cup (120milliliters) water

1/2 teaspoon garlic (granulated)
1/8 teaspoon clove powder (ground)
1/8 teaspoon cumin powder
3/4 cup (5 1/4 ounces or 150 grams) plums
(seedless, dried) aka prunes packed tightly
in your measuring cup
4 tablespoons (1/4 cup) honey
4 tablespoons (1/4 cup) white or apple cider
vinegar

1. Set the IP to SAUTE. Once HOT, add the sesame oil and onion; sauté till the edges start to brown, occasionally stirring. In a mixing bowl (small) or measuring cup (2-cup), add the vinegar, honey, water, and tomato puree using the measuring lines as a guideline. Add the cumin, clove, liquid smoke, hot sauce, garlic, and sauce; stir to mix very well. Add the vinegar mixture to the pot. Scrape any brown bits on the pot off using a spatula. Add the plums.
2. Lock the lid and close the pressure valve. Set to HIGH PRESSURE for 10 minutes. QPR gradually when the timer beeps; unlock the lid and open. Puree the mixture using an immersion blender till blended and smooth. Serve.

# Fresh Cooked Tomato Ketchup

Servings | **3 cups**    Prep. Time | **5 minutes**    Cook Time | **15 minutes**

**Nut. Content (per 1 tablespoon.):** Cal | **6.8**    Fat | **0.1g**    Protein | **0.1g**    Carbs | **1.7g**

1 tablespoon honey

1 tablespoon paprika

1 teaspoon salt

1/2 teaspoon mustard (Dijon)

1/3 cup raisins

1/4 teaspoon celery seeds

1/8 onion, wedged

1/8 teaspoon cinnamon

1/8 teaspoon clove powder

1/8 teaspoon garlic powder

2 pounds tomatoes (plum), quartered

6 tablespoons vinegar (apple cider)

Optional:

1 tablespoon of water

1 tablespoon cornstarch

1. Put all the ingredients in the IP, except for the optional water and cornstarch. With a potato masher, squish everything till enough juices come out of the tomatoes; they will not truly mash since they are not cooked yet. Mash till you get a 2-cup worth of juices.

2. Lock the lid and close the pressure valve. Set to HIGH PRESSURE for 5 minutes. QPR when the timer beeps; unlock the lid and open. Set the IP to SAUTE; let come to a simmer. Cook for 10 minutes uncovered.

3. If using a slurry of water and cornstarch, pour the mixture in the tomato mixture. Puree till smooth using an immersion blender. Transfer to a fresh-cleaned jar or glass bottle and seal. Let cool and keep refrigerated. It will last for around 6 months in the freeze and for 12 months if freezing in a freezer bag.

# Olive and Eggplant Spread

Servings|**4 - 6**    Prep. Time|**5 minutes**    Cook Time|**18 minutes**
**Nut. Content (per serving):** Cal|**155.5**    Fat|**11.7g**    Protein|**2g**    Carbs|**16.8g**

1 cup water
1 lemon, juiced (around 1/4 cup)
1 tablespoons tahini
1 teaspoon salt
1/4 cup black olives, pitted, reserve a couple un-pitted pieces to garnish
2 pounds (1 kilogram) eggplant

3 to 4 garlic cloves, skin on, reserve 1 clove to use fresh after cooking
4 tablespoons olive oil
A couple sprigs thyme (fresh), or 1 tablespoon leaves)
Olive Oil (extra-virgin), fresh

1. Peel alternating strip of no skin and skin on the eggplant. Slice the largest lengthwise chunks possible to cover the bottom of the IP. You can chop the rest pieces.
2. Set eh IP to SAUTE NORMAL mode. Add the olive oil. Once hot, put the large eggplant chunks in the pot with the face under; fry for 5 minutes or till caramelized. Add the garlic with the skin still on them. Flip the eggplants. Add the remaining chopped eggplant, water, and salt.
3. Lock the lid and close the pressure valve. Set to HIGH PRESSURE for 5 minutes. QPR when the timer beeps; unlock the lid and open.  Take the insert to the sink, tip over most of the cooking liquid over to remove and discard. Remove the garlic and peel the skin.
4. Add the black olives, garlic cloves (uncooked and cooked), lemon juice, and tahini in the insert; puree using an immersion blender. Transfer to a serving dish. Garnish with thyme and remaining olives. Drizzle with fresh olive oil just before serving.

# MEATY DISHES (PORK, BEEF, GOAT & LAMB)

### Shredded Hawaiian Pork

Servings | **4 to 6**    Prep. Time | **15 minutes**    Cook Time | **60 minutes**
**Nut. Content (per 6 serving):** Cal | **573**    Fat | **15.5g**    Protein | **40.5g**    Carbs | **25.4g**

Sauce:
1 tablespoon chili sauce
1 tablespoon ginger (fresh), minced
1/2 cup pineapple juice (reserved)
1/2 teaspoon Chinese-5 spice blend
15-ounces (canned) pineapple chunks packed with juice, reserve juice
2 tablespoons honey
2 tablespoons soy sauce
3 cloves garlic, peeled & minced

Pork:
1 cup pineapple juice (reserved)
1 teaspoon salt
1/2 teaspoon pepper
2 tablespoons olive oil
3 green onions, crosswise sliced
3 to 4 pounds pork (shoulder/butt), sliced 4 to 5-inch portions
Hawaiian rolls & coleslaw to serve

1. Sauce: Open the pineapple can. Drain the juice in a bowl (small); set aside. Reserve the pineapple for later.
2. In a saucepan (small), mix the spice blend, chili sauce, ginger, garlic, honey, soy sauce, and 1/2 cup pineapple juice. Cook on medium-high flame/heat till thick; set aside.
3. Pork: Set the IP to SAUTE. Add the olive oil; spread to coat the bottom of your pot. Once HOT, add the pork in batches to prevent overcrowding the pot; cook for 3 to 4 minutes without disturbing. Flip them over and sear the other side.
4. Once all the pork is brown and in the pot, press CANCEL. Add 1 cup pineapple juice; scrape the brown bits off the pot. Lock the lid and close the pressure valve. Set to HIGH PRESSURE for 60 minutes. NPR for 10 minutes when the timer beeps and QPR; unlock the lid and open.
5. Transfer the pork to a serving plate using tongs. Shred the meat using 2 forks; remove any large chunks of fat. Season with extra pepper and salt as needed. Pour the sauce over the meat, top with the pineapple chunks, and garnish with green onion. Serve.

# Mississippi Pot Roast

Servings|4    Prep. Time|**15 minutes**    Cook Time|**45 minutes**
**Nut. Content (per serving):** Cal|**0**    Fat|**0g**    Protein|**0g**    Carbs|**0g**

1 tablespoon cornstarch
2 tablespoons (1 packet) dressing mix (dry Ranch)
2 tablespoons (1 packet) dry mix au jus
2 tablespoons olive oil

3 pounds beef (chuck roast_
4 tablespoons butter
4 to 8 pepperoncini, adjust to preference, plus more to serve
Parsley, chopped to serve

1. Set the IP to SAUTE. Add the olive oil. Once HOT, add the beef; let cook for 6 to 8 minutes without disturbing till the underside is brown. Flip and cook for 5 minutes or till the other side is brown. Press CANCEL.

2. Spread the butter on top of the meat. Sprinkle with the Ranch and au jus. Top with the pepperoncini and the water around the meat. Lock the lid and close the pressure valve. Set to MEAT/STEW for 45 minutes.

3. NPR for 20 minutes when the timer beeps and QPR; unlock the lid and open. Transfer the pepperoncini and the beef and to a serving plate. Shred the beef into large chunks using 2 forks.

4. Set the IP to SAUTE; let the cooking juices come to a boiling. Mix 1 tablespoon water with the cornstarch till smooth in a bowl (small). Once boiling, add the slurry while constantly whisking; mix till thick. Pour the sauce over the meat. Serve garnished with parsley. Top with pepperoncini if desired.

# Rice & Red Beans w/ Andouille Sausage

Servings|**6**    Prep. Time|**10 minutes**    Cook Time|**60 minutes**
**Nut. Content (per serving):** Cal|**421**    Fat|**14.2g**    Protein|**23.37g**    Carbs|**53.2g**

Rice:
1/2 teaspoon salt
1 cup white rice (uncooked)

Parsley, chopped to garnish

Sausage & red beans:
1 clove garlic, minced
1 cup red beans (dried)
1 medium bell pepper (green), seeded & diced
1 pound andouille sausage, cooked & sliced
1 teaspoon oregano (dried)

1 teaspoon salt
1/2 onion (medium) diced
1/2 teaspoon cayenne pepper
2 stalks celery, sliced
3 cups water

1. Rice: Put all of the ingredients in the IP; stir to mix and level the rice. Lock the lid and close the pressure valve. Set to RICE and let cook to automatic time. QPR when the timer beeps; unlock the lid and open. Fluff the rice using a fork. Transfer the rice to a bowl (large), garnish with the parsley; set aside. Wash the inner pot and dry well.

2. Sausage & red beans: Put all of the ingredients in the IP; stir to mix well. Lock the lid and close the pressure valve. Set to HIGH PRESSURE for 45 minutes. NPR for 10 minutes when the timer beeps and QPR; unlock the lid and open. Stir to mix well. Serve with the rice.

# Sweet & Spicy Asian Ribs

Servings | **4**    Prep. Time | **15 minutes**    Cook Time | **25 minutes**
**Nut. Content (per serving):** Cal | **732**    Fat | **26.4g**    Protein | **74.18g**    Carbs | **45.9g**

Sauce:
1 tablespoon ginger (fresh), minced
1 tablespoon Hoisin Sauce
1/2 cup ketchup
1/2 cup soy sauce
1/2 cup sugar
1/2 teaspoon flakes red pepper
2 cloves garlic, minced
3 tablespoons honey

Ribs:
2 tablespoons sliced green onions, to garnish
1/2 cup vinegar
1 tablespoon sesame seeds, to garnish
1 tablespoon salt
1 tablespoon pepper
1 rack (2 to 3 pounds) ribs (baby back), sliced into half to fit the IP

1. Sauce: Mix all of the ingredients in a saucepan (small). Set on medium flame/heat. Whisk till the sugar dissolves and the sauce thickens.
2. Ribs: Remove the rib membrane if still on; season them with pepper and salt generously. Brush the meaty sides with 2 ounces of the sauce.
3. Put the IP trivet in the inner pot and pour the water and vinegar. With the meaty side under, arrange the ribs on the trivet, overlapping the pieces as needed.
4. Lock the lid and close the pressure valve. Set to HIGH PRESSURE for 25 minutes. Meanwhile, turn on your oven to broil. Set a baking rack on a rimmed sheet pan. NPR for 10 minutes when the timer beeps and QPR; unlock the lid and open.
5. With tongs, transfer the ribs to the prepared baking rack with the meaty side above. Slather them with the rest of the sauce. Place the sheet pan 4 inches from the heat source; broil for 5 to 10 minutes or till charred nicely. Remove from the oven; top with green onions and sesame seeds.

# Braised Bistro-Style Short Ribs & Mushrooms

Servings|**3**    Prep. Time|**20 minutes**    Cook Time|**90 minutes**
**Nut. Content (per serving):** Cal|**627**    Fat|**35g**    Protein|**58.3g**    Carbs|**22.5g**

1 1/4 tablespoon butter, divided, bring half of it to temperature
1 3/4 pounds mushrooms (brown cremini), thinly sliced
1 3/4 pounds short ribs beef (boneless)
1 bay leaf
1 teaspoon thyme (dried)
1 thin bacon strip, chopped

1/2 cup wine (dry red, such as Cabernet Sauvignon
1/2 red onion (small) chopped (1/4 cup)
1/2 teaspoon sage (dried)
1/4 cup broth (chicken or beef)
1/4 teaspoon black pepper (ground)
1/4 teaspoon salt (table)
3/4 tablespoons flour (all-purpose)

1. Set the IP to SAUTE for 35 minutes. Add 1/2 tablespoon butter in the pot; let melt. Add the bacon; fry for 4 minutes or till crisp, occasionally stirring. Transfer to a bowl (large) using a slotted spoon. Add 1/2 of the ribs. Cook for 10 minutes or till all the sides are well browned, occasionally turning. Transfer to the bowl with the bacon. Cook the rest of the ribs in the same manner; transfer to the bowl, too.

2. Add the onion in the pot; sauté for 3 minutes or till soft. Add the mushrooms; cook for 5 minutes or till their moisture cooks off. Add the wine; scrape the brown bits off the pot. Press CANCEL. Stir in the bay leaves, pepper, salt, thyme, and broth. Add the bacon and ribs, along with any meat juices; stir to mix well.

3. Lock the lid and close the pressure valve.  Set to HIGH PRESSURE for 1 hour & 30 minutes. Cancel the KEEP WARM mode and unplug when the timer beeps. NPR for 10 to 15 minutes or till the indicator is down and QPR; unlock the lid and open.

4. Discard the bay leaves. Transfer the ribs, bacon, and any veggie to a serving plate using a slotted spoon or tongs; cover with foil to keep warm. Skim the fat off from the sauce.

5. Set the IP to SAUTÉ for 5 minutes. Let come to a simmer. Mix the flour and the melted butter till smooth. Gradually add the flour mixture in the pot while stirring the sauce; whisk for 1 to 2 minutes or till smooth. Press CANCEL. Pour the sauce over the veggies and meat. Serve.

## Braised Italian-Inspired Meatballs

Servings|**3**   Prep. Time|**10 minutes**   Cook Time|**12 minutes**
**Nut. Content (per serving):** Cal|**386**   Fat|**17.2g**   Protein|**37.9g**   Carbs|**17.4g**

1 cup broth (chicken or beef)
1 small egg
1 teaspoon basil or oregano (dried)
1/2 carrot (medium), thinly sliced (1/4 cup)
1/2 medium bell pepper (green or red) stemmed, cored, & chopped (1/2 cup)
1/2 pound bulk Italian sausage (mild or sweet, no casings)
1/2 pound ground beef (lean)

1/2 teaspoon thyme (dried)
1/2 yellow onion (small), chopped (1/4 cup)
1/4 cup dried breadcrumbs (Italian-seasoned)
1/4 teaspoon salt (table)
1/8 cup milk (low-fat or regular)
1/8 teaspoon nutmeg (grated)
14-ounce (canned) diced tomatoes

1. Stir the bell pepper, tomatoes, carrot, onion, broth, nutmeg, salt, thyme, and oregano/basil in the IP. In a bowl (large), mix the milk, breadcrumbs, egg, sausage, and beef till uniformly mixed. Using dry, clean hands, scoop a scant 1/4-cup of the mixture and shape into balls, making around 6 balls.
2. Gently submerge the balls into the tomato sauce. Lock the lid and close the pressure valve. Set to HIGH PRESSURE for 1 hour & 30 minutes. Cancel the KEEP WARM mode and unplug when the timer beeps. NPR for 10 to 15 minutes or till the indicator is down and QPR; unlock the lid and open. Serve in serving bowls with plenty of sauce.

# Brisket Skewers

Servings | **2 to 3**    Prep. Time | **10 minutes**    Cook Time | **50 minutes**
**Nut. Content (per serving):** Cal | **256**    Fat | **12.5g**    Protein | **34.6g**    Carbs | **1.3g**

1 3/4-ounce (1/2 bottle) liquid smoke
1 cup water
1 pound lean (first-cut or flat) brisket, cubed into 1 1/2-inch chunk
1/2 tablespoon paprika (mild smoked)

1/2 teaspoon onion powder
1/4 teaspoon garlic powder
1/4 teaspoon salt (table)
6 to 8 pieces 4-inch metal or bamboo skewers 4-inch

1. Toss the beef cubes with the salt, garlic powder, onion powder, and paprika in a bowl (large) till thoroughly and evenly coated. Thread 2 cubes onto each skewer.
2. Put the water and the liquid smoke in the pot; set a trivet on the bottom. Pile the skewers on the trivet. Lock the lid and close the pressure valve. Set to HIGH PRESSURE for 50 minutes. Cancel the KEEP WARM mode and unplug when the timer beeps. NPR for 10 to 15 minutes or till the indicator is down and QPR; unlock the lid and open.
3. Heat a grill (cast-iron, large) on medium-high flame/heat till smoking. Brush with oil and prepare for direct cooking on high heat. Grill the skewers for 2 minutes or till brown and crisp, occasionally turning. Serve with BBQ sauce, regular salsa, or salsa verde for dipping.

# Tandoori  Pork Ribs BBQ

Servings | **4**    Prep. Time | **5 minutes**    Cook Time | **20 minutes**
**Nut. Content (per serving):** Cal | **361**    Fat | **12.88g**    Protein | **48.2g**    Carbs | **8.7g**

1 1/2 teaspoons salt
1/2 cup preferred BBQ Sauce
1-inch ginger, roughly chopped
2 bay leaves
2 pounds (1 kilogram) Pork Baby Back or Short-Ribs

3 cups water, or as needed
4 tablespoons Tandoori Spice Mix, or preferred rub
5 garlic cloves

1. Slice the ribs to that they will fit your IP. Place them in the pot as flat as possible. Add the salt, garlic, 2 tablespoons of tandoori, ginger, and bay leaves. Add enough water to the ribs, around 4 cups.
2. Lock the lid and close the pressure valve. Set to HIGH PRESSURE for 18 to 22 minutes. Cancel the KEEP WARM mode and unplug when the timer beeps. NPR for 10 to 15 minutes or till the indicator is down and QPR; unlock the lid and open.
3. Carefully transfer the ribs to a slicing board. Cover it with some foil; let sit for around 5 minutes to cool. Pat them dry and then brush with the BBQ sauce or tandoori paste. At this point, you can wrap them with the foil and keep refrigerated for up to 3 days. Barbecue, broil, and grill for 5 minutes each side. Serve right away.

# Pot Roast Italian Ragu

Servings|**1 pound**    Prep. Time|**10 minutes**    Cook Time|**85 minutes**
**Nut. Content (per 1/4 pound):** Cal|**203**    Fat|**10.2g**    Protein|**24.5g**    Carbs|**4.9g**

1 pound beef chuck (boneless) fat trimmed, halved
1 tablespoon olive oil
1 teaspoon oregano (dried)
1/2 bay leaf
1/2 medium garlic clove peeled & minced (1 teaspoon)
1/2 tablespoon capers, drained & rinsed, chopped

1/2 tablespoon rosemary (dried)
1/4 cup frozen pearl onions (do not thaw)
1/4 teaspoon black pepper (ground)
1/4 teaspoon salt (table)
14 ounces (canned) whole tomatoes
6 tablespoons red wine (light dry), such as Pinot Noir

1. Set the IP to SAUTE for 20 minutes. Add the oil; heat for 1 to 2 minutes. In batches as needed, cook the beef in the pot till well browned, flipping a few times. Transfer to a bowl when done.
2. Wash your hands and dry. Individually squeeze the tomatoes over the pot; add any remaining juice in the IP. Add the onion, stir to mix well; scrape the brown bits of the pot. Saute for 2 minutes or till the onions are light brown, stirring often. Press CANCEL.
3. Stir in the pepper, salt, bay leaf, oregano, rosemary, garlic, capers, and wine. Add the browned beef and any meat juice. Lock the lid and close the pressure valve. Set to HIGH PRESSURE for 55 minutes. Cancel the KEEP WARM mode and unplug when the timer beeps.
4. NPR for 10 to 15 minutes or till the indicator is down and QPR; unlock the lid and open. Skim the fat off the sauce. Discard the bay leaf. Shred the meat right in the pot using tongs or 2 forks.
5. Set the IP to SAUTÉ for 10 minutes; let the sauce come to a simmer. Cook for 5 minutes or till reduced to ragu texture, stirring occasionally. Stir 2 tablespoons butter before serving. Pairs well with fusilli or rigatoni, or you can also serve this as a stew on large spoonfuls of ricotta. Garnish with minced fresh parsley leaves.

# Carnitas

Servings|**3**    Prep. Time|**10 minutes**    Cook Time|**35 minutes**
**Nut. Content (per serving):** Cal|**668**    Fat|**45.2g**    Protein|**58.5g**    Carbs|**3.3g**

1 1/2 pounds pork butt (boneless & skinless) fat removed, meat chunked into 2-inch cubes
1 tablespoon preferred cooking fat
1 teaspoons cumin (ground)
1/2 teaspoon salt (table)

1/4 cup lime marmalade
1/8 packed cup basil leaves (fresh), chopped
3 medium cloves garlic, peeled & minced (1 tablespoon)
3/4 cups broth (chicken)

1. Whisk the marmalade, broth, salt, cumin, garlic, and basil in the IP till the marmalade dissolves. Add the pork; stir to mix well. Lock the lid and close the pressure valve. Set to HIGH PRESSURE for 40 minutes. Cancel the KEEP WARM mode and unplug when the timer beeps. NPR for 10 to 15 minutes or till the indicator is down and QPR; unlock the lid and open.
2. Transfer the pork to a slicing board (large) using tongs. De-fat the sauce. Set the IP to SAUTÉ for 10 minutes; let the sauce come to boil. Cook for 6 to 7 minutes or till the texture is similar to barbecue sauce, stirring often. Press CANCEL. Pour the sauce to a small heatproof serving bowl.
3. Heat the cooking oil in a skillet (large) over medium heat. Add enough pork that will not overcrowd the skillet; cook for around 5 minutes or till crisp and brown, occasionally turning. Transfer to a serving plate. Ladle the sauce over the pork. Serve pico de gallo, sour cream, and corn or flour tortillas.

# Pulled Brisket

Servings | **4**    Prep. Time | **20 minutes**    Cook Time | **1 hour, 45 minutes**
**Nut. Content (per serving):** Cal | **398**    Fat | **26g**    Protein | **27g**    Carbs | **14g**

1 1/2 pound beef brisket (preferably flat cut), trimmed & cut widthwise into half
1 garlic cloves (medium), peeled & minced (2 teaspoons)
1 tablespoon vinegar (balsamic), pomegranate molasses
1/2 tablespoon leaves thyme (fresh)
1/4 cup pearl onions (frozen, do not thaw)

1/4 cup wine (bold red, such as Syrah or Zinfandel), or 1/4 cup beef broth & 1 teaspoon sugar (dark brown)
1/4 teaspoon black pepper (ground)
1/4 teaspoon salt (table)
3 green olives (large) pitted & sliced
4 carrots (baby)
4 prunes (pitted), or raisins for a sweet sauce
7 ounces (canned) diced tomatoes

1. Mix the vinegar, wine, and tomatoes in the IP. Stir in the carrots, onion, prunes, thyme, olives, pepper, and salt. Nestle the meat on top of the sauce; turn them over to coat both sides with the sauce. Lock the lid and close the pressure valve. Set to HIGH PRESSURE for 1 hour and 30 minutes. NPR when the timer beeps; unlock the lid and open.

2. Transfer the meat to a chopping board using tongs. Skim the fat off from the surface of the sauce. Set the IP to SAUTÉ for 15 minutes. Let the sauce come to a simmer, stirring occasionally. Cook for 5 to 10 minutes or till the texture is a wet, loose barbecue sauce. Meanwhile, shred the beef using 2 forks or slice into thick pieces using a knife.

3. When the sauce is cooked to preferred consistency, stir the beef; cook for 1 minute, stirring till coated. Turn OFF the SAUTE. Remove the inner pot from the housing. Cover the pot partially; let set for5 minutes to meld the flavors and allow the meat to absorb the sauce. Serve over mashed potatoes, or with potato rolls with pickled jalapeno rings or pickle relish.

NOTES: Check the meat after pressure cooking. If you cannot shred it easily, PRESSURE COOK on HIGH for 10 minutes and NPR when the timer beeps.

# Fork-Tender Pork Ribs

Servings|**4**  Prep. Time|**10 minutes**  Cook Time|**35 minutes**
**Nut. Content (per 3 ribs):** Cal|**298**  Fat|**13g**  Protein|**22g**  Carbs|**20g**

1 rack (3 to 4 pounds) pork ribs

For the IP:
1/2 tablespoon Worcestershire sauce
1/3 cup water
2 tablespoons (apple cider or white wine) vinegar

For broiling/grilling:
5 tablespoons preferred barbecue sauce

Dry rub:
1 1/2 teaspoon chili powder
1 teaspoon black pepper (ground)
1 teaspoon cayenne pepper
1 teaspoon garlic powder
1 teaspoon onion powder
1 teaspoon paprika (smoked)
1 to 1 1/2 tablespoon salt
3 tablespoons sugar (brown)

1. Mix everything for your dry rub. Line a sheet pan with foil; lay the ribs on it, placing them upside down. With a paper towel, remove the thin membrane from the back of the ribs if desired. You can just leave them on. Generously rub the ribs with the spice mixture. Cover with foil; refrigerate for 30 to 60 minutes.
2. Pour all the ingredients for the IP in the pot. Coil the ribs to fir the inner pot. Lock the lid and close the pressure valve. Set to HIGH PRESSURE for 28 minutes or for 30 minutes for very tender meat. NPR for 10 minutes or QPR when the timer beeps; unlock the lid and open.
3. Transfer the ribs to a sheet pan. Coat the ribs with the BBQ sauce. Set a rack to the second groove of the oven. Place the pan on the rack; broil for 2 to 5 minutes on the presentation side. Or grill the ribs for the same time.

# Spicy Ground Meat & Peas

Servings | **4**    Prep. Time | **5 minutes**    Cook Time | **20 minutes**
**Nut. Content (per serving):** Cal | **408**    Fat | **30g**    Protein | **22g**    Carbs | **10g**

1 cup peas (frozen)
1 onion (small), chopped finely
1 pound preferred ground meat: turkey, lamb, chicken, or beef
1 tablespoon garlic & ginger paste, 3 cloves garlic & 1/2-inch ginger
1 teaspoon paprika
1 teaspoon salt
1 teaspoons cumin (ground)

1/2 teaspoon chili powder (red)
1/2 teaspoon turmeric powder
2 tablespoons cilantro (freshly chopped) to garnish
2 tablespoons olive oil
2 teaspoons garam masala
3 tablespoons tomato paste
3 teaspoons coriander powder
3/4 cup water, divided

1. Set the IP to SAUTE. After 30 seconds, add the oil, onion, and garlic & ginger paste; sauté for 1 minute. Add all the dry spices and salt; sauté for 30 seconds. Add 1/4 cup of the water and 3 tablespoons of the tomato paste; stir and sauté for 30 seconds. Add the meat and the rest of the water. Break the meat into smaller chunks using a long-handled spatula or wooden spoon; mix well.
2. Lock the lid and close the pressure valve. Set to HIGH PRESSURE for 10 minutes. QPR when the timer beeps; unlock the lid and open. Set the IP to SAUTE. Add the peas; saute for 1 to 2 minutes or till the excess liquid cooks off and the peas are cooked through. Turn OFF the IP. Stir in the cilantro; serve.

## Ethiopian-Style Beef Stew

Servings|4    Prep. Time|5 minutes    Cook Time|30 minutes
**Nut. Content (per serving):** Cal|461    Fat|25g    Protein|47g    Carbs|8g

1 1/2 pounds (stew meat) beef
1 onion (large), chopped finely
1 tablespoon garlic & ginger, crushed, 2 cloves garlic & 1/2-inch ginger or 1/2 teaspoon ginger powder & 1/2 teaspoon garlic powder
1 tablespoon onions (fried), optional
1 teaspoon salt, or as needed
1/2 teaspoon sugar
3 tablespoons butter or ghee
3 tablespoons tomato paste
1 cup water, divided

Spice mix (substitute with 1 to 1 1/2 tablespoons berbere seasoning if available & 2 teaspoons coriander powder).
1 tablespoon coriander powder
1 tablespoon garam masala
1 teaspoon cumin (ground)
1/4 teaspoon black pepper
1/4 teaspoon cayenne pepper
1/4 teaspoon nutmeg (ground)
1/4 teaspoon turmeric powder
2 teaspoon paprika (smoked)

1. Set the IP to SAUTE. After 30 seconds, add the ghee/butter, onion, garlic, ginger, salt, and turmeric; sauté for 1 minute or till lightly caramelized. Add 1/4 cup water, tomato paste, and all the dry spices; stir for 1 minute. Add the beef and rest of the water.
2. Press CANCEL. Lock the lid and close the pressure valve. Set to MEAT/STEW for 30 minutes. NPR when the timer beeps; unlock the lid and open. Adjust the seasonings as needed. Add the sugar. Serve with couscous & lemon vinaigrette dressed garden salad, or sourdough flatbread.

# Lamb Curry

Servings|**4**    Prep. Time|**10 minutes**    Cook Time|**20 minutes**
**Nut. Content (per serving):** Cal|**271**    Fat|**15g**    Protein|**24g**    Carbs|**6g**

1 onion (medium), chopped
1 pound leg steak lamb, chunked into 1-inch cubes
1 tablespoon olive oil (light)
1 teaspoon paprika
1 teaspoon salt adjust to preference
1/2 cup yogurt (plain) or coconut milk
1/2 teaspoon cardamom powder
1/2 teaspoon lime juice to garnish before serving

1/2 teaspoon turmeric powder
1/4 teaspoon cayenne pepper
2 tablespoon garlic & ginger, grated (6 cloves garlic & 1-inch ginger)
2 tablespoons cilantro (fresh), chopped to garnish
2 tablespoons tomato paste
3 teaspoons garam masala adjust to preference
3/4 cup water, divided

1. Set the IP to SAUTE. After 30 seconds, add the oil, onion, and garlic & ginger paste; sauté for 1 minute. Add 1/4 cup water, tomato paste, and all the spices; stir to mix well.
2. Add the lamb, rest of the water, and coconut milk; stir to mix well. Lock the lid and close the pressure valve. Set to HIGH PRESSURE for 12 to 15 minutes. NPR for 15 minutes when the timer beeps and QPR; unlock the lid and open. Serve garnished with cilantro and drizzle with the lime juice. Serve with cauliflower rice, brown rice, cumin basmati rice, flatbread, or naan.

# Ground Meat Naan Pizza

**Servings | 4    Prep. Time | 10 minutes    Cook Time | 30 minutes**
**Nut. Content (per serving):** Cal | **702**    Fat | **44g**    Protein | **35g**    Carbs | **40g**

Meat:

1 onion (small), chopped finely
1 pound ground lamb, beef, chicken, or turkey
1 tablespoon garlic & ginger paste, 3 cloves garlic & 1/2-inch ginger
1 teaspoon paprika
1 teaspoon salt
1 teaspoons cumin (ground)
1/2 teaspoon chili powder (red)

1/2 teaspoon turmeric powder
2 tablespoons olive oil
2 teaspoons garam masala
2 to 3 tablespoons cilantro (fresh), chopped to garnish
3 tablespoons tomato paste
3 teaspoons coriander powder
3/4 cup water, divided

Naan Pizza:

1 1/2 cups bell peppers (red, preferred color, or a mixture), sliced
1 1/2 cups mozzarella cheese, shredded
Pinch Cayenne for sprinkling on top, optional

1 tablespoon cilantro (fresh), to top
1 tablespoon Olive oil (extra-virgin) & 1 crushed clove garlic, microwaved for 20 seconds
4 Naan (whole-wheat or regular)

1. Meat: Set the IP to SAUTE. After 30 seconds, add the oil, onion, and garlic & ginger paste; sauté for 1 minute. Add the salt and all the spices; sauté for 30 seconds. Add 1/4 cup of water and 3 tablespoons tomato paste; stir for 30 seconds. Add the rest of the water and the meat; break the meat using a spatula or wooden spoon and mix well.
2. Lock the lid and close the pressure valve. Set to HIGH PRESSURE for 10 minutes for beef and lamb or for 8 minutes for chicken and turkey. QPR when the timer beeps; unlock the lid and open. Set the IP to SAUTE. Add the peas; cook for 1 to 2 minutes till the remaining liquid is gone. Turn the IP off.
3. Pizza: Crush the garlic and add it to the olive oil. Microwave for 20 seconds. Chop the peppers. Once the oil is infused with the garlic, remove the clove and discard. Brush the naan with the garlic oil. Spread around 1/3 to 1/2 cup cheese, an even layer of meat, and sliced peppers for each naan. Season with cayenne and cilantro. Bake for 8 minutes in a preheated 425 oven or till the cheese is melted and the base of the naan is nicely toasted. Let rest for 5 minutes before slicing.

# Goat Curry

Servings | **6**    Prep. Time | **10 minutes**    Cook Time | **20 minutes**
**Nut. Content (per serving):** Cal | **557**    Fat | **46**    Protein | **27g**    Carbs | **5g**

Marinade: (Mix till well blended)

1 1/2 teaspoon salt, adjust to preference, add after cooking
1 onion (medium), sliced thin
1 tablespoon coriander powder
1 tablespoon paprika
1 teaspoon turmeric powder
1/2 cup cilantro, chopped
1/2 teaspoon cayenne, adjust to preference, optional

2 pounds mutton or young goat (bone-in), sliced into 1-inch chunks (goat or lamb meat will work), pat dry
2 tablespoons garlic & ginger paste, 1-inch ginger PLUS 6 cloves garlic, chopped finely or grated
2 tablespoons olive oil (light) or oil (vegetable)
2 teaspoons to 1 tablespoon garam masala

Curry:

1 cup yogurt (plain), whisked till smooth before adding
2 gold potatoes (medium), cubed into 2-inch chunks
2 tablespoons ghee or olive oil (light)

Garnish:

1/2 teaspoon cardamom powder, or seeds from 5 to 6 pods, crushed

1. Put all the marinade ingredients in a mixing bowl or a 1-gallon resealable bag; mix till well combined. If possible, marinate in the fridge for 1 hour or so.
2. Set the IP to SAUTE MORE mode. Add the oil. Once HOT, add the marinated meat; sauté for 3 to 4 minutes, stirring once. Add the potatoes and yogurt; stir well and scrape the brown bits off the pot. The meat juices and the yogurt will have released enough liquid for pressure cooking. If not, add water as needed. Lock the lid and close the pressure valve.  Set to MEAT for 15 minutes. NPR for 15 minutes when the timer beeps and QPR; unlock the lid and open.
3. To thicken break some of the potatoes using a wooden spoon. Set the IP to SAUTÉ; cook for 2 to 3 minutes. The gravy will thicken as it cools. Turn the IP off. Add the cardamom; stir to mix. Serve with rice or naan and yogurt-cucumber dip.

# Lentils & Pork Sausage

Servings|**4**    Prep. Time|**5 minutes**    Cook Time|**15 minutes**
**Nut. Content (per 6 servings):** Cal|**378**    Fat|**29g**    Protein|**18g**    Carbs|**12g**

1 1/2 cups lentils (dry), rinsed
1 bay leaf
1 onion (large), chopped
1 tablespoon butter
1 tablespoon olive oil

1, 500 grams Cotechino or 1 pound pork sausage (fresh country) in casings
2 celery stalks, chopped
2 cups stock (vegetable)
Salt to taste

1. Rinse your pork sausage clean. Poke holes all over the casing and put them in the IP steamer basket. Set the IP to SAUTE. Once HOT, add the olive oil, butter, and onion; sauté for 5 minutes or till the onion starts to soften. Add the celery, sauté for 1 minute. Mix in the lentils, bay leaf, and stock. Set the basket with your sausage on top of the lentil layer.
2. Lock the lid and close the pressure valve. Set to HIGH PRESSURE for 10 to 12 minutes. NPR for 10 minutes when the timer beeps and QPR; unlock the lid and open.
3. Remove the basket with the sausage. Taste the lentil mixture and mix in enough salt as needed. Discard the bay leaf. Scoop the lentils to a serving plate with a slotted spoon. Slice the sausage; arrange them on top of the lentils. Serve with some mashed potatoes.
NOTES: You can add 2-inch cubes of potatoes in the basket with the sausage and cook it together with the dish.  Mash the cooked potatoes and mix with some salt and milk for a quick mashed potato dish.

# Sloppy Joes & Tangy Slaw

Servings|**6 - 8**    Prep. Time|**10 minutes**    Cook Time|**25 minutes**
**Nut. Content (per serving):** Cal|**179.8**    Fat|**5.9g**    Protein|**15g**    Carbs|**18g**

Sloppy Joes:
1 1/2 teaspoons salt
1 carrot, grated
1 cup (250 milliliters) tomatoes, chopped, canned with their juice or fresh
1 cup (250 milliliters) water
1 medium bell pepper (red or green), chopped
1 pound (500 grams) ground beef (extra lean), frozen or fresh

1 red onion (medium), chopped
1 tablespoon olive oil
1 tablespoon Worcestershire sauce, optional
1/2 cup (45 grams) rolled oats
2 teaspoons garlic powder
4 tablespoons (80 grams) tomato paste
4 tablespoons vinegar (apple cider)

Tangy coleslaw:
1 tablespoon honey
1 tablespoon mustard (grainy Dijon)
1/2 head cabbage, quartered & thinly sliced (around 5 cups)

1/2 red onion, chopped finely
2 carrots, grated (around 1 cup)
2 tablespoons vinegar (apple cider)

1. Sloppy Joe: Set the IP to SAUTE. Once HOT, add the oil and ground meat. Cook each side of the slab for 8 minutes or till brown. Push the beef aside to one side of the pot. Add the carrots, peppers, onion, garlic powder, and salt to the cleared portion; sauté for 5 minutes or till the veggies are soft.
2. Add the water, tomato paste, chopped tomatoes, vinegar, and Worcestershire; stir to mix well. If the frozen meat is soft, break it to chunks. Scrape any brown bits from the pot. Let come to a boil. Once boiling, add the oats on top of the meat mixture – DO NOT STIR.
3. Lock the lid and close the pressure valve. Set to HIGH PRESSURE for 10 minutes. QPR gradually when the timer beeps; unlock the lid and open. Set the IP to SAUTE; cook for 5 minutes or till the cooking liquid is slightly reduced, breaking and mixing the ground meat in the process. Let stand for 5 minutes to thicken before serving.
4. Coleslaw: Mix the honey, vinegar, and mustard in a bowl (large), whisking well. Mix in the carrots, cabbage, and onions. Serve with the sloppy Joe.

# Silky Beef-Porcini Mushroom Stew

Servings|**4 - 6**    Prep. Time|**5 minutes**    Cook Time|**20 minutes**
**Nut. Content (per 6 servings):** Cal|**334.9**    Fat|**15.7g**    Protein|**32.2g**    Carbs|**10.1g**

1 celery stalk, sliced into 1/2-inch pieces
1 cup (250milliliters) stock (beef) (salt-free)
1 ounce (30 grams) porcini mushrooms (dried), rinsed
1 red onion (medium), roughly diced
1 sprig rosemary, stems removed & chopped finely (around 1 teaspoon)
1 tablespoon olive oil
1 teaspoon salt (reduce if using butter & salted stock)

1/2 cup (125 milliliters) red wine, such as Sangiovese, Chianti, or any non-sweet tart red
1/4 teaspoon pepper
2 carrots (large), cut into 1/2-inch thick coins
2 pounds (1 kilogram) beef chuck, cubed into 1-inch chunks
2 tablespoons butter (unsalted)
2 tablespoons flour (all-purpose)

1. Set the IP to SAUTE. Once HOT, add the oil and beef; sear one side of the meat for 5 minutes. Add the pepper, salt, stock, wine, celery, onions, and rosemary; stir to mix well. Add the carrots and mushrooms on top of the meat mixture. Lock the lid and close the pressure valve. Set to HIGH PRESSURE for 20 minutes.

2. Meanwhile, melt the butter in a pan (small). Add the flour; mix till the texture is paste-like. Cook till the butter starts to bubble in the flour.

3. QPR when the timer beeps; unlock the lid and open. Scoop around 6 tablespoons of the cooking liquid into the pan with butter mixture to loosen the paste. Add the mixture to the pot; stir to mix well. Set the IP to SAUTÉ; let come to a simmer. Cook for 5 minutes or till thick.

# Pork Carnitas

Servings | **3 to 4**     Prep. Time | **10 minutes**     Cook Time | **30 minutes**
**Nut. Content (per serving):** Cal | **546**     Fat | **38g**     Protein | **44g**     Carbs | **6.6g**

1 bay leaf
1 tablespoon cumin
1 teaspoon coriander powder
1 teaspoon Mexican or regular oregano
1 teaspoon paprika
1 teaspoon salt
1 to 1 1/2 pounds pork shoulder or butt, sliced into 3-inch chunks, or use ribs (country style)

1/2 cinnamon stick, around 2 to 3-inch long
1/2 onion (small), chopped
1/3 cup orange juice
1/4 teaspoon pepper
1/8 teaspoon cayenne powder (use 1/4 teaspoon or more for spicier)
2 tablespoons olive oil
2 teaspoon chili powder
4 cloves garlic, minced or pressed

1. Mix the cayenne, coriander, oregano, paprika, chili powder, cumin, pepper, salt, and oil in a mixing bowl till well combined. Add the pork in the spice mixture; toss to coat all the sides.
2. Set the IP to SAUTE MORE mode. Once HOT, add the pork; cook till all the sides are brown, but not cooked through. Transfer the meat to a bowl; set aside.
3. Add the cinnamon stick, bay leaf, and onion in the pot; cook till the onion is tender, occasionally scraping and stirring to remove the brown bits off the pot. Add a splash of water as needed to deglaze. Add the garlic; cook for a couple of seconds occasionally stirring. Add the orange juice; stir. Return the meat, just nestling them down into the juice – they will not be covered.
4. Lock the lid and close the pressure valve. Cancel SAUTÉ. Set the IP to HIGH PRESSURE for 30 minutes. QPR when the timer beeps; unlock the lid and open. Skim off the excess fat settling on top of the liquid using a small measuring cup or spoon; discard. Stir the ingredients. Transfer to a serving dish.
5. Drain the carnitas a bit if serving them in tacos. The sauce is flavorful so use it. If desired, transfer the carnitas to a sheet pan, and broil them in the oven at 450F till crisped to desired preference. Serve garnished with avocado, cheese, cilantro, salsa, sour cream, and tortillas.

# GRAINS & BEANS

## Split Pigeon Pea Curry

Servings|**6**    Prep. Time|**10 minutes**    Cook Time|**10 minutes**
**Nut. Content (per serving):** Cal|**72**    Fat|**2g**    Protein|**2g**    Carbs|**9g**

1 cup split pigeon peas, rinsed & soaked in warm water
1 onion (small), sliced or chopped
1 tablespoon ghee or butter
1 teaspoon coriander powder
1 teaspoon garam masala
1 teaspoon mustard seeds (black)
1 teaspoon salt
1 to 2 green chili, optional

1 tomato (medium), diced
1/2 teaspoon cayenne powder, adjust to preference
1/2 teaspoon turmeric powder
1-inch ginger, crushed or chopped finely
2 cups water
2 tablespoons cilantro, chopped
3 cloves garlic, crushed or chopped finely
6 to 8 leaves curry or 2 leaves kaffir lime

1. Rinse the lentils and then soak in water. Rinse and strain before using. Set the IP to SAUTE. After 30 seconds, add the oil and mustard seeds. Once sizzling, add the onion, chili, and curry leaves; sauté for 30 to 45 seconds or till the onion turns pink. Add your garlic and your ginger; fry for around 30 seconds. Add the tomato, salt, and spices; sauté for 30 seconds.
2. Add the peas and 2 cups water; stir to mix well. Lock the lid and close the pressure valve. Set to HIGH PRESSURE for 6 minutes or for 8 minutes or a mushy texture. NPR for 10 minutes when the timer beeps and QPR; unlock the lid and open. Add the cilantro. Serve.

## Brown Rice

Servings|**4**    Prep. Time|**1 minute** Cook Time|**30 minutes**
**Nut. Content (per 3/4 cup):** Cal|**108.2**    Fat|**0.9g**    Protein|**2.5g**    Carbs|**22.4g**

2 cups (500 milliliters) brown rice

2 1/2 cups (625 milliliters) water

1. Carefully measure your ingredients and put them in the IP. Even the layer by stirring the content with your fingers. Lock the lid and close the pressure valve. Set to HIGH PRESSURE for 20 minutes. NPR for 10 minutes when the timer beeps and QPR; unlock the lid and open. Fluff the rice using a fork; serve.

## Brown Rice (Jasmine)

Servings | **4**    Prep. Time | **5 minutes**    Cook Time | **25 minutes**
**Nut. Content (per serving):** Cal | **180**    Fat | **2g**    Protein | **3g**    Carbs | **36g**

1/2 teaspoon salt
1 teaspoon olive oil
1 cup water & 2 tablespoons, for a softer texture
1 cup rice (brown jasmine)

1.  Turn ON the IP. Add all the ingredients; stir to mix and even the rice layer. Lock the lid and close the pressure valve. Set to HIGH PRESSURE for 22 minutes. NPR when the timer beeps; unlock the lid and open. Fluff the rice using a fork.

## Cumin Basmati Rice

Servings | **3**    Prep. Time | **5 minutes**    Cook Time | **15 minutes**
**Nut. Content (per serving):** Cal | **240**    Fat | **2g**    Protein | **4g**    Carbs | **49g**

1 cup & 2 tablespoons water
1 cup rice (Basmati), rinsed 2 to 3 times & soaked for 20 minutes

1 teaspoon ghee, butter, or oil
1/2 teaspoon cumin seeds
1/2 teaspoon salt adjust to preference

1. Strain the rice after soaking. Turn the IP to SAUTE. After 30 seconds. Add the cooking fat and cumin seeds. Once the seeds are sizzling, add the rice; sauté for 30 seconds. Add the water and salt; stir to mix.
2. Lock the lid and close the pressure valve. Set to HIGH PRESSURE for 6 minutes. NPR for 10 minutes when the timer beeps and QPR; unlock the lid and open. Fluff the rice using a fork. Best served warm with preferred grilled entrée, curries, or lentil soups.
NOTES: You can actually just mix all the ingredients in the IP and pressure cook it. The dish will only have a milder cumin flavor if you do it this manner.

## Saffron Rice Pilaf

Servings|**4**    Prep. Time|**5 minutes**    Cook Time|**16 minutes**
**Nut. Content (per serving):** Cal|**233**    Fat|**5g**    Protein|**4g**    Carbs|**41g**

1 cup rice (Basmati or Jasmine)
1 cup water
1 teaspoon ghee or oil
1/2 teaspoon saffron, soaked in 1 tablespoon hot water or microwaved with the water for 20 to 30 seconds

1/2 teaspoon salt
2 tablespoons almonds (slivered), optional

Optional ingredients:
1 tablespoon raisins
1 tablespoon cashews

1. Rinse the rice 2 to 3 times or till the water runs clear. If possible, soak them in water for 15 minutes and drain. Put the saffron in a microwavable bowl; break them down into small pieces. Add 1 tablespoon hot water. Or add cold water if microwaving it.
2. Put the rice in the IP. Add the rest of the ingredients. Lock the lid and close the pressure valve. Set to HIGH PRESSURE for 6 minutes or to RICE for 12 minutes. NPR for 10 minutes when the timer beeps and QPR; unlock the lid and open. Fluff the rice using a fork. Serve.

## Chickpeas

Servings|**6**    Prep. Time|**8 hours**    Cook Time|**15 minutes**
**Nut. Content (per serving):** Cal|**120**    Fat|**2g**    Protein|**6g**    Carbs|**22g**

1 cup chickpeas (dry), soaked overnight in 4 cups of water
1/2 teaspoon salt
3 cups water

1. You can soak the peas or leave them unsoaked. Rinse them well either way. Add to the pot. Add the water and salt. Lock the lid and close the pressure valve. Set to HIGH PRESSURE for 15 minutes for soaked or for 40 minutes for unsoaked chickpeas. NPR for 10 to 15 minutes when the timer beeps and QPR; unlock the lid and open.
2. Strain the chickpeas; save the cooking liquid as stock for stews, curries, and soups. Store the chickpeas in the fridge for up to 1 week.

## Spinach Rice Pilaf

Servings|6    Prep. Time|**20 minutes**    Cook Time|**25 minutes**
**Nut. Content (per serving):** Cal|**163**    Fat|**3g**    Protein|**3g**    Carbs|**29g**

1 cup rice (Basmati), rinse 2 to 3 times, soak for 20 minutes if possible
1 cup water
1 onion (small) or 2 shallots, chopped or thinly sliced
1 tablespoon garlic and ginger, crushed or grated (1/2-inch ginger & 3 cloves garlic)
1 teaspoon coriander (ground)
1 teaspoon cumin seeds
1/2 lime juiced (around 1 teaspoon), to add after cooking

1/2 teaspoon garam masala (store-bought or homemade)
1/4 to 1/2 teaspoon chili powder (red)
2 tablespoons cashews, or slivered almonds (blanched)
2 teaspoons butter or ghee
2 to 3 tablespoons cilantro (fresh), chopped
3/4 teaspoon salt adjust to preference
6 ounces baby spinach (bagged), chopped finely

1. Rinse your rice till clear. Soak for 20 minutes in water if possible. Rinse and drain before using.
2. Set the IP to SAUTE. Add the ghee. Once heated, add the cumin seeds; wait for them to sputter and sizzle, around 15 to 20 minutes. Add the cashews and onion; add the green chilies and curry leaves with them if using. Sauté for 30 seconds. Add your garlic and your ginger; fry for around 30 seconds.
3. Add the cilantro and spinach; sauté for 1 minute or till the spinach is wilted. Add the rice; sauté for 1 minute. Add the water and spices. Lock the lid and close the pressure valve. Set to HIGH PRESSURE for 6 minutes.
4. NPR for 5 minutes when the timer beeps and QPR; unlock the lid and open. Fluff the rice using a fork. Let stand uncovered for 5 minutes. Drizzle with lime juice; gently mix. Serve.

## Quinoa & Rice

Servings|**4 - 6**    Prep. Time|**1 minute** Cook Time|**13 minutes**
**Nut. Content (per serving):** Cal|**101.6**    Fat|**0.6g**    Protein|**2.8g**    Carbs|**20.7g**

1 3/4 cups (340 grams) rice (Basmati) (dry)
3 cups (750 milliliters) water
5 tablespoons (70 grams) quinoa (black or red), rinsed

1. Put the quinoa, rice, and water in the IP. Lock the lid and close the pressure valve. Set to HIGH PRESSURE for 3 minutes. NPR for 10 minutes when the timer beeps and QPR; unlock the lid and open. Fluff using a fork and serve.

# Kidney and Black Bean Curry

Servings | **4**    Prep. Time | **8 hours**    Cook Time | **30 minutes**
**Nut. Content (per serving):** Cal | **229**    Fat | **7g**    Protein | **10g**    Carbs | **30g**

Beans:
3 cups water
1/4 cup kidney beans (red)
1/2 cup black gram

Curry:
1 cup onion, chopped, around 1 medium
piece
1 cup tomatoes, crushed, or 2 Roma
tomatoes (medium), pureed
1 tablespoon butter
1 tablespoon ginger, crushed or 1-inch
ginger, crushed or grated
1 teaspoon cumin seeds
1 to 2 green chilies, tops chopped
3 cloves garlic, crushed or chopped finely

Spices:
1 teaspoon chili powder (Kashmiri red) or
paprika
1/4 teaspoon cayenne
1/4 teaspoon turmeric powder
2 cups water
2 teaspoon coriander (ground)
2 teaspoon garam masala
3/4 teaspoon salt, adjust to preference

After cooking:
1 teaspoon butter, optional
1/4 teaspoon garam masala
2 tablespoon cilantro, chopped
2 tablespoons cream (heavy whipping)

1. Wash the beans. Soak in 4 cups water for at least hours up to overnight. Strain and rinse well before using; set aside.
2. Set the IP to SAUTE. Add the cumin seeds; cook till sizzling. Add the onions; sauté for 1 minute. Add the pureed tomatoes; scrape the brown bits off the pot. Add all the spices, lentils, and 2 cups water. Lock the lid and close the pressure valve. Set to HIGH PRESSURE for 30 minutes. NPR when the timer beeps; unlock the lid and open.
3. Mash using a potato masher to make the curry creamier. Add the butter, cream, garam masala; let stand for a couple of minutes. Garnish with cilantro; serve.

## Basic Risotto

Servings | **4**     Prep. Time | **5 minutes**     Cook Time | **12 minutes**
**Nut. Content (per serving):** Cal | 374     Fat | 18g     Protein | 21g     Carbs | 54g

1 onion, chopped
1 swig wine (white)
1 tablespoon parmesan cheese
2 cups rice (Arborio or short grain white pearl)

4 cups (1 liter) broth (vegetable or chicken)
Olive oil (extra-virgin)
Salt and pepper to taste

1. Set the IP to SAUTE. Once HOT, add the oil and onion; sauté for 5 minutes or till the onion is translucent. Add the rice; toast lightly to release the starch. Stir and cook till some of the grains are golden and toasted.
2. Add the wine; scrape any stuck rice off the pot. Stir to mix well. Add the broth; stir to mix. Lock the lid and close the pressure valve immediately. Set to HIGH PRESSURE for 5 to 6 minutes. Cancel the KEEP WARM mode, unplug, and QPR when the timer beeps; unlock the lid and open. Remove the inner pot from the housing to prevent the rice from overcooking.
3. The risotto will appear to be slightly too wet. Stir for around 30 seconds or till the rice absorbs the extra liquid. If the mixture is still too wet, return the inner pot to the housing. Set the IP to SAUTE LESS mode or KEEP WARM and let evaporate till desired consistency is reached. To make a classic dish, stir in 1 tablespoon butter and grated cheese in the risotto just before serving.

## 1-Minute Quinoa

Servings | **4**     Prep. Time | **10 minutes**     Cook Time | **10 minutes**
**Nut. Content (per serving):** Cal | 186     Fat | 3g     Protein | 7.5g     Carbs | 34g

1 1/2 cups water
1 bell pepper (yellow), finely diced
1 bunch parsley or cilantro, roughly chopped
1 cucumber, seeded & finely diced

1 cup black quinoa, rinsed
1 lime, zested & squeezed
Pinch salt
1 Roma tomato (large), finely diced
1/2 cup green olives, chopped

1. Add the quinoa, water, salt, and lime zest in the IP. Lock the lid and close the pressure valve. Set to HIGH PRESSURE for 1 minute. NPR for 10 minutes when the timer beeps and QPR; unlock the lid and open.
2. Transfer the quinoa to a mixing bowl and let cool. Add the cilantro, cucumber, olives, pepper, and tomato. Drizzle with the lime juice; stir to mix. Adjust seasoning as needed. Serve at room temperature or chilled.

## Refried Beans

Servings|0    Prep. Time|**5 minutes**    Cook Time|**15 minutes**
**Nut. Content (per serving):** Cal|**383**    Fat|**4.8g**    Protein|**21.9g**    Carbs|**64g**

1 bunch cilantro or parsley, stems & leaves divided, chopped
1 onion, chopped
1 tablespoon oil (vegetable), bacon fat, lard, or preferred fat
1 teaspoon salt

1/2 teaspoon cumin
1/4 teaspoon chipotle powder
2 cups cranberry, pinto, or borlotti beans, or a mixture (dried), soaked
2 cups water

1. Set the IP to SAUTE. Once HOT, add the oil and onion, cumin, chipotle, and parsley stems; sauté till the onion is just turning soft. Add the beans and water. Lock the lid and close the pressure valve. Set to HIGH PRESSURE for 7 to 10 minutes. Cancel the KEEP WARM mode and unplug when the timer beeps. NPR for 10 to 15 minutes or till the indicator is down and QPR; unlock the lid and open.
2. Scoop out 1 heaping spoonful of bean mixture as garnish. Sprinkle the rest with salt and mash with a potato masher till desired texture is achieved. Garnish with the whole beans, parsley, and an optional scoop of sour cream, yogurt (plain) (from whole milk).

## Coconut Rice

Servings|**4**    Prep. Time|**5 minutes**    Cook Time|**6 minutes**
**Nut. Content (per serving):** Cal|**280**    Fat|**12g**    Protein|**4g**    Carbs|**38g**

1 cup coconut milk
1 cup rice (white long-grain), such as Jasmine or Basmati
1/4 teaspoon salt

1. Rinse the rice well and put in the pot. Add the coconut milk and salt. Lock the lid and close the pressure valve. Set to HIGH PRESSURE for 6 minutes. NPR for 10 minutes when the timer beeps and QPR; unlock the lid and open. Gently fluff the rice using a fork.

## Cumin Millet Pilaf

Servings | **4 -6**    Prep. Time | **5 minutes**    Cook Time | **15 minutes**
**Nut. Content (per 6 servings):** Cal | **100.8**    Fat | **3.1g**    Protein | **2.4g**    Carbs | **16.3g**

1 bay leaf
1 tablespoon ghee or oil (vegetable)
1 teaspoon cardamom (crushed), around 3 whole pods or 1/4 teaspoon powder)
1 teaspoon salt

1 white onion (large), halved & cut into strips
1-inch cinnamon stick
2 cups millet (decorticated organic)
3 cups water
3 teaspoons cumin seeds

1. Set the IP to SAUTE. Once HOT, add the oil, cinnamon stick, cardamom, cumin, and bay leaf; sauté for 1 minute or till the cumin starts to crackle. Add the onion; sauté for 5 minutes or till soft. Add the millet; stir to coat with the oil well. Add the salt and water.
2. Lock the lid and close the pressure valve. Set to HIGH PRESSURE for 1 minute. Cancel the KEEP WARM mode and unplug when the timer beeps. NPR for 10 to 15 minutes or till the indicator is down and QPR; unlock the lid and open. Fluff the millet; serve.

## Sushi Rice

Servings | **around 18 sushi**    Prep. Time | **1 minute** Cook Time | **22 minutes**
**Nut. Content (per serving):** Cal | **188.7**    Fat | **0g**    Protein | **2.9g**    Carbs | **44.8g**

1 1/2 cups (375 milliliters) water
1 cup (200 grams) sushi rice
3 tablespoons vinegar (rice wine) or 1 tablespoon vinegar (apple cider) & Pinch sugar

1. Rinse the rice very well for 3 minutes or till the water runs clear, rubbing it in your strainer as the water passes through the grains. Transfer to the IP. Add the water; mix to distribute evenly in the pot.
2. Lock the lid and close the pressure valve. Set to HIGH PRESSURE for 7 minutes. NPR for 5 minutes when the timer beeps and QPR; unlock the lid and open.
3. Stir the vinegar into the rice, delicately mixing without over-mixing. Transfer the rice mixture to a wooden bowl (large) or a cutting board (wooden) and smooth into an even layer. Let cool for 10 minutes and use for making preferred sushi.

# Tasty Black Beans

Servings | **3 cups**    Prep. Time | **10 minutes**    Cook Time | **35 minutes**
**Nut. Content (per serving):** Cal | **388**    Fat | **13.5g**    Protein | **23g**    Carbs | **46g**

1 1/2 teaspoons Mexican or 1 teaspoon oregano
1 bay leaf (small)
1 cup black beans (dry), sorted & rinsed
1 teaspoon chili powder
1/2 onion (small), diced
1/2 teaspoon coriander powder
1/2 teaspoon paprika (smoked)
1/4 teaspoon black pepper
1/4 teaspoon salt (kosher), or 1/8 teaspoon salt (table), or 1/4 teaspoon if not using bacon)
2 teaspoon cumin

3 cloves garlic, finely minced or pressed
3 cups broth (vegetable or chicken), preferably low-sodium
3 slices bacon, chopped, preferably thick, lean slices

Garnish:
Cilantro (fresh)
Cotija or preferred cheese
Hot sauce
Salsa
Sour cream

1. Set the IP to SAUTE NORMAL mode. Once HOT, add the bacon; cook and stir till almost done. Scoop out any excess fat. Add the onion; cook and stir for a few minutes. Add the bay leaf, garlic, coriander, pepper, salt, chili powder, oregano, paprika, and cumin; stir often till fragrant – do not let the garlic burn. Add a bit of broth if the pot seems too hot. Add the broth; stir to mix. Add the beans; stir to mix.
2. Lock the lid and close the pressure valve. Cancel SAUTÉ. Set to MANUAL HIGH PRESSURE for 35 minutes. NPR for 15 minutes when the timer beeps and QPR; unlock the lid and open. Taste and adjust salt as needed. Garnish as preferred and serve.
NOTES: Omit the bacon and use a vegetable broth to make this vegetarian. Sauté the onion with a bit of olive oil first before continuing with the recipe. If you want to cook this as a soup, add 1/4 cup more of broth. You can even add some chopped celery and carrots, too.

# Perfect Quinoa

Servings | **2 - 4**    Prep. Time | **5 minutes**    Cook Time | **21 minutes**
**Nut. Content (per serving):** Cal | **172**    Fat | **2.8g**    Protein | **6g**    Carbs | **3g**

1 1/2 cup (375 milliliters) water
1 cup (175 grams quinoa

Pinch salt, optional

1. Put the quinoa in a strainer (fine-mesh). Rinse under running water for a couple of minutes, rubbing the grains together using your hands. Transfer to the IP. Add the water and salt. Lock the lid and close the pressure valve. Set to HIGH PRESSURE for 1 minute. Cancel the KEEP WARM mode and unplug when the timer beeps. NPR for 10 to 15 minutes or till the indicator is down and QPR; unlock the lid and open. Fluff the quinoa; serve.

## Sorghum Risotto

Servings | **4 - 6**    Prep. Time | **10 minutes**    Cook Time | **25 minutes**
**Nut. Content (per 6 servings):** Cal | **537.8**    Fat | **15.8g**    Protein | **15.5g**    Carbs | **93.7g**

1 1/2 cups (350 milliliters) sorghum
1 tablespoon olive oil
1 teaspoon salt
1 white onion (medium), chopped

1/2 cup tomatoes (sun-dried), roughly diced
2 1/4 cups (625milliliters) water
2 zucchini (medium), grated
3 sprigs thyme (fresh), reserve 1 to garnish

1. Set the IP to SAUTE. Once HOT, add the olive oil and onion; sauté till soft. Add the sorghum; stir to coat with the oil and onion. Toast for 3 minutes. Add the tomatoes, zucchini, water, salt, and thyme; stir to mix well.
2. Lock the lid and close the pressure valve. Set to HIGH PRESSURE for 13 minutes. NPR for 10 minutes when the timer beeps and QPR; unlock the lid and open. Mix well so some of the zucchini is broken and the mixture is creamy.

# VEGAN

## Tabbouleh Quinoa Salad

Servings|4    Prep. Time|0 minutes    Cook Time|30 minutes
**Nut. Content (per serving):** Cal|185    Fat|11g    Protein|3g    Carbs|18g

Salad:
1 cup cherry tomatoes, chopped
1 cup parsley, chopped finely
1 cup quinoa (cooked)
1/4 cup pomegranate seeds, optional
1/4 cup red onion, chopped finely
2 cups English or Persian cucumber, chopped
2 tablespoons mint, chopped

Dressing:
1/2 teaspoon salt (adjust to preference)
1/4 black pepper (fresh ground)
3 tablespoons lemon juice
3 tablespoons olive oil (extra-virgin)

1. Prepare the quinoa following package directions. Around 1/3 cup of uncooked grains produces 1 cup when cooked. Rinse the quinoa and transfer to the IP. Add 1 cup water and 1/4 teaspoon salt. Lock the lid and close the pressure valve. Set to HIGH PRESSURE for 2 minutes. NPR for 10 minutes when the timer beeps and QPR; unlock the lid and open.
2. Transfer the quinoa in a mixing bowl (large). Add the cucumbers, tomatoes, onions, and herbs. Mix the dressing ingredients in a small bowl or Mason jar till well combined. Pour the dressing over the salad; mix well. You can add some pomegranate seeds in the bowl if desired; toss well. Serve cold.

## Rice (Basmati) Confetti

Servings|4 - 6    Prep. Time|5 minutes    Cook Time|13 minutes
**Nut. Content (per serving):** Cal|271.3    Fat|2.9g    Protein|5.5g    Carbs|54.8g

1 bell pepper (medium, preferred color)
1 carrot, grated
1 onion (medium), chopped
1 tablespoon olive oil

1 teaspoon salt
1/2 cup (65 grams) peas (frozen or fresh)
2 cups (500milliliters) long-grain or Basmati
Water as needed

1. Set the IP to SAUTE NORMAL mode. Once HOT, add the olive oil and onion; sauté till translucent. Meanwhile, in a 1-liter or 4-cup measuring cup, add the grated carrots and bell pepper; pat down lightly into an even layer. Add enough water in the cup to reach the 3-cup level; set aside.
2. Add the peas, rice, and salt in the IP; stir to mix well. Add the veggies and water of the measuring cup in the pot; stir to mix well. Lock the lid and close the pressure valve. Set to HIGH PRESSURE for 3 minutes. NPR for 10 minutes when the timer beeps and QPR; unlock the lid and open. Fluff the rice; serve.

## Lentil Risotto

Servings|**4 -6**   Prep. Time|**5 minutes**   Cook Time|**15 minutes**
**Nut. Content (per 6 servings):** Cal|**190**   Fat|**2.5g**   Protein|**5.7g**   Carbs|**35.1g**

1 celery stalk, chopped
1 cup lentils (dry), soaked overnight
1 cup rice (Arborio)
1 onion (medium), chopped
1 tablespoon olive oil

2 garlic cloves, mashed lightly
2 sprigs parsley, leaves & stems chopped
(around 1 tablespoon)
3 1/4 cups (750milliliters) stock (vegetable)

1. Set the IP to SAUTE. Once HOT, add the oil and onion; sauté till they begin to soften. Add the celery and parsley; sauté for 1 minute. Add the rice and the garlic; stir to mix well. Cook for 1 minute till evenly moistened and pearly. Add the stock and the lentils; stir to mix well.
2. Lock the lid and close the pressure valve. Set to HIGH PRESSURE for 5 minutes. QPR when the timer beeps; unlock the lid and open. Stir to mix well and serve. Drizzle with olive oil (extra-virgin).
3. NOTES: You can add 1 medium potato, diced into 1/2-inch chunks, into the cooker along with the stock to make the dish heartier and create a classic recipe.

## Black Bean Chili

Servings|**4**   Prep. Time|**5 minutes**   Cook Time|**25 minutes**
**Nut. Content (per serving):** Cal|**225**   Fat|**4g**   Protein|**12g**   Carbs|**45g**

1 onion (medium) chopped
1 pack taco seasoning, adjust to preference
1 tablespoon olive oil
1/2 bell pepper (green), chopped
1/2 cup corn (frozen)
14 ounces (canned) diced or crushed tomatoes

16 ounces (canned) black beans, rinsed & drained
2 teaspoon cocoa powder (unsweetened), optional, but recommended
3/4 cup water, use 1/2 cup if cooking chili for nachos
4 ounces (canned) diced (fire-roasted) mild green chilies

1. Set the IP to SAUTE. Once HOT, add the olive oil, green pepper, and onions; sauté for 1 minute. Add the taco seasoning; stir for 30 seconds. Add everything else; mix well. If short on time, just mix all the ingredients in the pot.
2. Lock the lid and close the pressure valve. Set to HIGH PRESSURE for 8 minutes. NPR for 10 minutes or QPR when the timer beeps; unlock the lid and open.
3. Adjust seasoning as needed; let cool for 5 minutes. Garnish as preferred, such as tortilla chips, avocado, sour cream, shredded cheese, cilantro, etc.

## Farro & Lentils

Servings|**1 to 2**    Prep. Time|**2 minutes**    Cook Time|**12 minutes**
**Nut. Content (per 2 servings):** Cal|**372**    Fat|**2.2g**    Protein|**19.5g**    Carbs|**66.4g**

Lentils:

1/4 teaspoon paprika (smoked)

1/4 teaspoon onion powder

1/4 teaspoon garlic powder

1/4 teaspoon cumin powder

1/4 teaspoon black pepper

1/2 teaspoon salt

1/2 teaspoon oregano (dried)

1/2 teaspoon chili powder (medium)

1/2 teaspoon basil (dried)

1/2 cup lentils (brown, black, or green)

1 1/4 cup stock (vegetable) or water

Farro:

1/2 teaspoon salt

1/2 teaspoon onion powder

1/2 teaspoon Italian herbs

1/2 cup farro

1 cup water

1. Put all of the ingredients in the IP. Set the IP trivet on top of the mixture. Put the farro ingredients in a heatproof bowl (small, stainless steel). Put the bowl on the trivet.
2. Lock the lid and close the pressure valve. Set to HIGH PRESSURE for 12 minutes. NPR when the timer beeps; unlock the lid and open. Serve with preferred sauce and veggies.

## Carrots & Green Beans

Servings|**4**    Prep. Time|**10 minutes**    Cook Time|**5 minutes**
**Nut. Content (per serving):** Cal|**72**    Fat|**5g**    Protein|**1g**    Carbs|**5g**

1 cup carrots, chopped into 1/2-inch chunks

1 cup green beans, sliced into 1/2-inch pieces

1 tablespoon olive oil

1/2 teaspoon mustard seeds

1/2 teaspoon salt

1/2 teaspoon turmeric

1/4 cup PLUS 2 tablespoons water, or as needed

1/4 teaspoon cayenne, adjust to preference

2 tablespoon coconut flakes (unsweetened)

2 teaspoon coriander powder

1. Prepare the veggies before cooking. Set the IP to SAUTE. Add the oil. Once HOT, add the mustard seeds. Once sizzling, add the carrots and beans; sauté for 30 seconds. Add the spices, salt, and water. Add the optional coconut flakes; stir to mix.
2. Cancel SAUTE. Lock the lid and close the pressure valve. Set to HIGH PRESSURE for 1 minute. QPR when the timer beeps; unlock the lid and open. Serve garnished with cilantro.

# Rice & Chickpea Curry

Servings|**4**    Prep. Time|**10 minutes**    Cook Time|**40 minutes**
**Nut. Content (per serving):** Cal|**458**    Fat|**11g**    Protein|**14g**    Carbs|**75g**

Chickpea curry:

1 1/4 cups water
1 cup chickpeas (dried), soaked overnight,
or 1 can chickpeas, rinsed & drained
1 onion (medium), sliced
1 tablespoon coriander powder
1 tablespoon garam masala
1 tablespoon garlic & ginger paste, 3 cloves
garlic & 1/2-inch ginger
1 tablespoon ghee or olive oil
1 teaspoon cumin seeds

1 teaspoon paprika (smoked)
1 teaspoon salt
1 tomato (large), chopped
1/2 teaspoon chili powder (red) or cayenne
pepper
1/2 teaspoon turmeric powder
2 green chilies (serrano0 or seeded
jalapeños for less spice
2 teaspoon cumin (ground)

Rice:

1 cup long-grain rice (Basmati), soaked &
rinsed
1/2 cup cilantro & mint, chopped
1/2 cup onions (fried)

1/2 teaspoon saffron soaked in 1
tablespoon warm-hot water
1/2 teaspoon salt

1. Prepare the rice and soak while you prepare all the veggies and make the chickpea curry.
2. Set the IP to SAUTE. Add the oil. Once heated, add the cumin seeds. When they start to sizzle, add the onions and chilies; sauté for 30 seconds. Add your garlic and your ginger; fry for around 30 seconds. Add the tomatoes and all the spices for the curry; stir to mix well and sauté for 30 seconds. Add the chickpeas; stir to mix well.
3. Lock the lid and close the pressure valve. Set to BEAN/CHILI for 25 minutes for soaked dried or for 6 minutes for canned chickpeas. QPR when the timer beeps; unlock the lid and open. Add the rice and the salt for the rice recipe. Top with the mint and cilantro, saffron with the soaking liquid, and onions. Gently press down using a spatula.
3. Lock the lid and close the pressure valve. Set to HIGH PRESSURE for 6 minutes. NPR when the timer beeps; unlock the lid and open. Fluff the rice using a fork. Serve with lemon vinaigrette dressed garden salad or spicy yogurt cucumber dip.

## Kidney Bean Curry

Servings | **4**    Prep. Time | **5 minutes**    Cook Time | **30 minutes**
**Nut. Content (per serving):** Cal | **128**    Fat | **4g**    Protein | **5g**    Carbs | **17g**

1 1/2 cups water
1 cup kidney beans (dried red), soaked overnight, or 1 can
1 onion (small), chopped finely
1 tablespoon garlic & ginger paste, 3 cloves garlic & 1/2-inch ginger
1 tablespoon olive oil (light) or ghee
1 teaspoon cumin seed
1 teaspoon roasted cumin (ground)

1 teaspoon salt adjust to preference
1 teaspoon turmeric powder
1/4 teaspoon cayenne pepper
2 green chilies (de-seeded or whole), optional
2 tablespoons cilantro, chopped to garnish
2 teaspoon coriander powder
2 teaspoon garam masala
2 tomatoes pureed, or 1 cup crushed

1. If using dried beans, rinse them and soak in water overnight. Rinse and drain before using. Set the IP to SAUTE MORE mode. After 30 seconds, add the oil, green chilies and cumin seeds. Once the seeds start to splutter, add the onion and garlic & ginger paste; sauté for 30 seconds. Add the crushed tomatoes and all of the spices; sauté for 30 seconds. Add the beans and water; stir to mix.
2. Lock the lid and close the pressure valve. Set to HIGH PRESSURE for 25 minutes. NPR when the timer beeps; unlock the lid and open. Serve garnished with the cilantro.

## Thai Green Tofu Curry

Servings | **4**   Prep. Time | **5 minutes**   Cook Time | **10 minutes**
**Nut. Content (per serving):** Cal | **360**   Fat | **23g**   Protein | **14g**   Carbs | **28g**

1 can coconut milk
1 cup baby corn, sliced
1 cup carrots (around 2 medium), chopped
1 pound tofu (extra-firm) cut into 1/2 to
3/4-inch cubes
1/2 of a 4-ounce can green curry paste
(Maesri Thai), or use the whole can
1/4 cup water

After cooking:
1 cup peas (frozen)
1/2 teaspoon lime juice
2 teaspoon Sugar (brown)
Basil leaves (Thai) or mint, to garnish

1. Set the IP to SAUTE. Add the water and the coconut milk. Add the curry paste; whisk to mix well. Add the carrots, corn, any preferred vegetable, and tofu; stir to mix. Let come to a simmer to prevent the milk from curdling. Lock the lid and close the pressure valve. Press CANCEL. Set to HIGH PRESSURE for 2 minutes. NPR for 5 minutes when the timer beeps and QPR; unlock the lid and open.

2. Adjust seasoning as needed. Add the lime juice and sugar. Add the peas. Let cook for 1 to 2 minute with the residual heat. If the sauce is thin, set the IP to SAUTÉ; cook for 1 to 2 minute. Serve with brown or white Jasmine rice.

# Spiced Cauliflower & Potato

Servings | **4**    Prep. Time | **10 minutes**    Cook Time | **10 minutes**
**Nut. Content (per serving):** Cal | **93**    Fat | **4g**    Protein | **2g**    Carbs | **12g**

1 cup potatoes (Yukon gold or red), sliced
1 tablespoon ghee or olive oil
1 teaspoon cumin powder, roasted
1 teaspoon cumin seeds
1 teaspoon garlic, chopped finely
1 teaspoon ginger, chopped finely
1 teaspoon salt
1 to 2 teaspoon coriander powder
1 tomato (medium), chopped

1/2 cup onion (1/2 medium), sliced
1/2 teaspoon garam masala
1/2 teaspoon turmeric powder
1/4 to 1/2 teaspoon cayenne
2 cups florets cauliflower
2 jalapeños or 2 green chilies, deseeded for a milder flavor
2 tablespoons cilantro, chopped, to garnish

1. Set the IP to SAUTE. Once HOT, add the cumin seeds. Once sizzling, add the potatoes, onions, and green chilies; sauté for 1 minute. Add your garlic and your ginger; fry for around 1 minute.
2. Add the tomato, spices, and salt; sauté for 2 minutes. Add the cauliflower; gently stir. Cancel SAUTE. Lock the lid and close the pressure valve. Set to HIGH PRESSURE for 0 to 1 minute, depending on the size of the potatoes and florets.
3. QPR when the timer beeps; unlock the lid and open. If there is still liquid in the bottom of the pot, set the IP to SAUTÉ for a few minutes. Serve garnished with cilantro.

## Lemon Rice & Lentils

Servings | **4**    Prep. Time | **6 minutes**    Cook Time | **16 minutes**
**Nut. Content (per serving):** Cal | **239**    Fat | **4g**    Protein | **5g**    Carbs | **45g**

1 cup PLUS 2 tablespoons water
1 cup rice (Basmati), soaked for 20 minutes, rinsed 2 to 3 times
1 lemon juice, add after cooking
1 teaspoon ginger (around 1/2 inch), grated
1 teaspoon mustard seeds (brown)
1 teaspoon olive oil, ghee, or butter
1/2 teaspoon cumin (ground)

1/2 teaspoon salt
1/2 teaspoon turmeric powder
10 to 12 curry leaves
2 tablespoons cashews, optional
2 teaspoon gram lentils (split black), rinsed & dried
3 green chilies (whole), slice the tops off

1. Soak, rinse, and drain the rice. Do the same with the lentils. Set the IP to SAUTE MORE mode. Once HOT, add the cooking fat, lentils, and mustard seeds. When the lentils are lightly golden and the mustard seeds splutter, add the cashews, curry leaves, green chilies, ginger, spices, and salt; sauté for 30 seconds.
2. Add the rice and water; stir to mix. Lock the lid and close the pressure valve. Set to HIGH PRESSURE for 6 minutes. NPR for 5 minutes when the timer beeps and QPR; unlock the lid and open. Add the lemon juice; fluff the rice using a fork; gently mixing the lemon juice.

## Potato Salad

Servings | **6 -8**    Prep. Time | **5 minutes**    Cook Time | **15 minutes**
**Nut. Content (per 8 servings):** Cal | **237.6**    Fat | **7.3g**    Protein | **4.8g**    Carbs | **40.4g**

1 bunch parsley stems & leaves, chopped finely
1 dash pepper (fresh ground)
1 teaspoon salt, adjust to preference
1/4 white (medium) or 1/2 red onion (medium), chopped finely (around 1/3 cup)

3 pounds (1 1/2 kilograms) Potatoes (red or new), diced large
3 to 4 tablespoons vinegar (white wine)
4-5 tablespoons Olive oil (extra-virgin)

1. Put the IP steamer basket in the inner pot and pour 1 1/2 cups water. Scrub the potatoes and wash them well. Slice into 1-inch chunks. Put them in the basket. Lock the lid and close the pressure valve. Set to HIGH PRESSURE for 5 minutes.
2. Meanwhile, chop the onion and put in a bowl (small). Add the vinegar, pepper, and salt to soften. Chop the parsley stems and the leaves. QPR when the timer beeps; unlock the lid and open.
3. Transfer the potatoes in the bowl with the onion. Add the olive oil; mix well. Serve right away or refrigerate overnight to chill.

# Chickpeas Curry

Servings|4　Prep. Time|**5 minutes**　Cook Time|**35 minutes**
**Nut. Content (per serving):** Cal|**128**　Fat|**4g**　Protein|**4g**　Carbs|**18g**

1 1/2 cups water, or as needed
1 bag black tea, for color (Indian Tea or English Breakfast), optional
1 cup chickpeas, rinsed & soaked for 8 to 10 hours, or use 14-ounces (canned)
1 onion (medium), sliced thin
1 tablespoon coriander powder
1 teaspoon cumin powder
1 teaspoon cumin seeds
1 teaspoon fennel powder, optional
1 teaspoon pomegranate powder
1 teaspoon salt adjust to preference
1 tomato (Roma), deseeded & chopped finely

1/2 teaspoon dry mango powder
1/4 teaspoon cayenne
2 green chilies, stem removed
2 tablespoons garlic & ginger paste, 1-inch ginger & 6 to 7 cloves garlic, ground in your food processor
2 teaspoon garam masala, adjust to preference
2 teaspoons ghee or olive oil (refined)

Garnish:
2 tablespoons cilantro chopped
Light drizzle lime juice

1. If using chickpeas (dried), rinse and soak in 4 cups of water for at least 8 hours or overnight. Strain and rinse before using. If using canned, rinse and strain before using.
2. Set the IP to SAUTE. Add the oil/ghee; heat for 30 seconds. Once heated, add the cumin seeds. Once they start spluttering, add the onion, garlic, and ginger; sauté for 1 minute. Add the chopped tomatoes; sauté for 1 minute. Add the chickpeas, spices, and water. If using, add the bag of black tea.
3. Lock the lid and close the pressure valve. Set to BEAN for 30 to 35 minutes or till the chickpeas cook to your preferred softness for dried or for 6 to 8 minutes for canned. NPR when the timer beeps; unlock the lid and open.
4. Remove the tea bag if using. Mash some of the beans using a wooden spoon or potato masher to make the curry thick or creamy. Serve garnished with the cilantro and light drizzle of lime juice. Serve with rice or naan.

# Mango & Kale Slaw w/ Chickpeas

Servings|**0**    Prep. Time|**5 minutes**    Cook Time|**5 minutes**
**Nut. Content (per serving):** Cal|**169**    Fat|**7g**    Protein|**6g**    Carbs|**22g**

1 cup mango, peeled & cubed
1 tablespoon vinegar (apple cider)
1 tablespoon olive oil (extra-virgin)
1 teaspoon cumin (ground)
1 teaspoon paprika
1/2 cup soycutash (frozen), peas, or corn, optional
1/2 teaspoon black pepper (ground)

1/2 to 3/4 teaspoon salt, adjust to preference
10 ounces (bagged) kale slaw mixture: kale, green and red cabbage, Brussels sprouts, & broccoli slaw
2 to 3 tablespoons slivered almonds (dry roasted)
3/4 cup chickpeas (cooked or canned), or pressure-cooked dry chickpeas

1. If using dry chickpeas, soak them overnight in water. Rinse and drain well before using. Add to the IP. Add 1 cup water and 1/2 teaspoon salt. Lock the lid and close the pressure valve. Set to BEAN/CHILI for 30 minutes. NPR when the timer beeps; unlock the lid and open. Reserve 3/4 cup of the cooked chickpeas for the slaw; use the rest for curries, soups, and salads. If using canned chickpeas, rinse and drain before using as well.
2. Set a skillet (wide) on the stovetop and heat on medium-high flame/heat. Add the olive oil, chickpeas, and seasonings; sauté for 30 seconds. If using frozen soycutash, add it now; sauté for 30 to 60 seconds. Turn the flame/heat off. Add the almonds and mango; stir to mix well. Serve warm or cold.

# Spiced Chickpea Curry

Servings | **6**    Prep. Time | **10 minutes**    Cook Time | **35 minutes**
**Nut. Content (per serving):** Cal | **140**    Fat | **2g**    Protein | **7g**    Carbs | **23g**

1 cup chickpeas (dried), rinsed &soaked for 8 to10 hours in 4 cups of water
1 onion (medium) chopped
1 tablespoon coriander powder
1 tablespoon garam masala, adjust to preference
1 tablespoon or 1-inch ginger, crushed
1 teaspoon chili powder (Kashmiri red) or paprika
1 teaspoon cumin powder
1 teaspoon cumin seeds
1 teaspoon salt, adjust to preference

1/2 teaspoon fennel powder, optional
1/4 teaspoon cayenne
2 cups water, or more to preference
2 green chilies, deseeded & ribs removed
2 Roma tomato, deseeded & chopped finely, or pureed
3 cloves garlic, crushed

Garnish:
1 teaspoon lemon juice
1 teaspoon cumin powder, roasted
2 tablespoons cilantro, chopped

1. You can use canned chickpeas if dried is not available. Whether using canned or soaked chickpeas (dried), rinse them well and strain before using.
2. Set the IP to SAUTE MORE option. Add the ghee or oil. Once heated, add the cumin seeds. Once the seeds begin to sputter, add the ginger, onion, garlic, green chilies, and tomato; sauté for 1 minute.
3. Add the chickpeas, spices, and water. Lock the lid and close the pressure valve. Set to MANUAL or BEAN for 35 minutes for soaked and for 5 to 6 minutes for canned chickpeas. NPR for 10 minutes when the timer beeps and QPR; unlock the lid and open.
4. Mash a couple of the beans using a wooden spoon or potato masher to make it thick and creamy. Serve garnished with the cumin and cilantro. Drizzle with lemon juice.

# Bean Burger

Servings|**8**    Prep. Time|**15 minutes**    Cook Time|**15 minutes**
**Nut. Content (per serving):** Cal|**345**    Fat|**12g**    Protein|**16g**    Carbs|**44g**

Patties:
1 cup bell peppers (preferably rainbow peppers), chopped finely
1 cup corn (frozen)
1 cup shredded cheese (Mexican blend) or preferred shredded cheese, use 2 tablespoons cornstarch or coconut flour instead for vegan
1 egg (large), whisked, use 1/2 cup Panko breadcrumbs instead for vegan
1/2 cup cilantro, chopped
2 tablespoons olive oil (light) for grilling your patties
3 to 4 tablespoons Panko breadcrumbs for coating patties, optional
30 ounces (2 cans) pinto beans, or 1 cup dried pinto beans, rinsed & soaked overnight
4 tablespoons taco seasoning mix

Taco seasoning (makes 4 tablespoons):
1 tablespoon paprika
1 teaspoon cumin powder
1 teaspoon oregano (Mexican)
1 teaspoon salt, adjust to preference
1/4 to 1/2 teaspoon cayenne pepper
2 tablespoons chili powder

Burger:
1 burger buns (preferably honey whole-wheat)
1 sliced cheese (pepper-jack)
A couple slices tomato
Lettuce (Romaine or Iceberg)

Spicy mayo sauce:
1 teaspoon vinegar (apple cider)
2 tablespoons ketchup
2 tablespoons mayonnaise
2 teaspoons honey or agave nectar
2 teaspoons sriracha

1. If using canned beans, rinse and drain before using – no need to cook. If using dry beans, rinse, soak overnight in 4 cups of water, and rinse before using. Put the soaked beans in the IP. Add 1 teaspoon salt, 1 teaspoon olive oil, and 1 1/2 cup water. Lock the lid and close the pressure valve. Set to BEANS for 30 minutes. NPR for 10 minutes when the timer beeps and QPR; unlock the lid and open. Drain the cooked beans.
2. Put the beans in a mixing bowl (large). Mash them gently using a potato masher or fork – do not turn them into a paste; you want them to hold together. Add veggies, cheese, and all the seasonings; stir to mix well. Add the egg or breadcrumbs; stir to mix well. Divide the mixture into 8 to 10 portions. Wet your palms; shape each portion into a round patty gently. If using a breadcrumb coating, coat them before setting aside.
3. Heat a skillet (large) over medium-high flame/heat. Add a few drizzles of olive oil. Add the patties; cook each side for 6 to 8 minutes or till golden. Mix all of the spicy mayo ingredients well; set aside.
4. With a little butter, toast or warm your buns (optional, but recommended). Spread the mayo on the bottom bun. Put 1 to 2 patties on them. Spread 1 to 2 teaspoon of mayo on the patty;

top with 1 cheese slice, tomato slices, and lettuce. Spread the top bun with the mayo and cover the lettuce. Serve.

## White Bean Warm Salad

Servings|**3**    Prep. Time|**10 minutes**    Cook Time|**12 minutes**
**Nut. Content (per serving):** Cal|**187**    Fat|**2.9g**    Protein|**10.4g**    Carbs|**31g**

3/4 cups great northern or cannellini beans (dried)
1/2 red onion (small), chopped (1/4 cup)
1/4 teaspoon salt (table)
1/8 cup & 1/2 tablespoon olive oil
1/8 loosely packed cup parsley leaves (fresh), chopped finely
1/8 teaspoon flakes red pepper

1 medium clove garlic (1 teaspoon), peeled & minced
1 tablespoons vinegar (white wine)
1 teaspoon capers, drained & rinsed, chopped finely
1 teaspoon leaves rosemary (fresh), chopped finely
Water, adjust as needed

1. Soak the beans in water for at least 8 hours to 12 hours maximum. Drain before using. Put the beans in the IP. Add enough water to submerge them under 2-inch of water; add 1 tablespoon oil. Lock the lid and close the pressure valve. Set to HIGH PRESSURE for 12 minutes.
2. Meanwhile, whisk the vinegar and remaining oil in a heatproof bowl (large) till smooth. Stir in the capers, garlic, parsley, onion, salt, red pepper, and rosemary. QPR when the timer beeps; unlock the lid and open.
3. Drain the cooked beans in a sieve set in your sink, shaking it to drain well. Transfer the beans in the bowl with your dressing; toss to mix well. Serve over a steak.

# Kamut, Arugula, & Orange Salad

Servings | **6 -8**    Prep. Time | **10 minutes**    Cook Time | **30 minutes**
**Nut. Content (per serving):** Cal | **126.9**    Fat | **8.6g**    Protein | **2.8g**    Carbs | **11.7g**

1 bunch (2 loosely packed cups) arugula (rocket), around 4 ounces or 125 grams
1 cup Kamut grains (whole)
1 tablespoon olive oil (extra-virgin, cold-pressed)
1 teaspoon salt
1 teaspoon oil (vegetable)

1/2 cup cheese ribbons (Pecorino Romano), optional
1/2 lemon
2 1/4 ounces (75 grams) walnuts (shelled), roughly chopped (around 1/2 cup)
2 blood oranges (medium), peeled, sliced crosswise & segments separated
2 cups water

1. Rinse the kamut. Transfer to a bowl (large). Add 4 cups water and juice of 1/2 a lemon. Let soak for 12 hours or overnight. Rinse and strain just before using.
2. Put the kamut in the IP. Add the oil, salt, and water. Lock the lid and close the pressure valve. Set to HIGH PRESSURE for 15 to 18 minutes. Cancel the KEEP WARM mode and unplug when the timer beeps. NPR for 10 to 15 minutes or till the indicator is down and QPR; unlock the lid and open. Strain the kamut and rinse under cold running water to cool down.
3. Transfer the kamut to a serving bowl. Add the olive oil, walnuts, orange segments, and arugula; toss to mix well. Garnish with the cheese if using. Store leftovers in a tightly-sealed container and keep refrigerated for several days.

## Caper & Beet Salad

Servings|**4 -6**    Prep. Time|**5 minutes**    Cook Time|**30 minutes**
**Nut. Content (per 6 servings):** Cal|**43.1**    Fat|**2.4g**    Protein|**0.7g**    Carbs|**5.4g**

2 tablespoons rice wine or vinegar (white balsamic)

4 beets (medium)

Dressing:
1 bunch parsley (small), stems removed (around 1 heaping tablespoon chopped)
1 garlic clove (large),
1 tablespoon olive oil (extra-virgin)

1/2 teaspoon salt
2 tablespoons capers
Pinch black pepper

1. Put the IP steamer basket in the inner pot and pour 1 cup water. Cut the tops off the beets. Clean the roots well, making sure you do not pierce the skin. Put them in the trivet. Lock the lid and close the pressure valve. Set to HIGH PRESSURE for 20 to 25 minutes.
2. Meanwhile, chop the parsley and garlic together. Transfer them to a jar (small) with a tight seal. Add the capers, olive oil, pepper, and salt. Close the lid; shake vigorously.
3. QPR when the timer beeps; unlock the lid and open. The beets are done when a fork easily pierces through them. Otherwise, PRESSURE COOK on HIGH for 5 minutes more. QPR when the timer beeps; unlock the lid and open.
4. Transfer the steamer from the pot to the sink under running cold water to cool the beets. With your hands (gloved or not) or a dull knife, brush the skin off.  Slice the beets crosswise into pieces. Arrange them on a serving plate. Sprinkle with the vinegar; they will keep for 4 days if stored tightly covered. Shake the dressing vigorously one more time. Pour over the beets just before serving.

# Spicy Citrus Cauliflower Salad

Servings|**4**　Prep. Time|**5 minutes**　Cook Time|**10 minutes**
**Nut. Content (per serving):** Cal|**317**　Fat|**16g**　Protein|**14g**　Carbs|**39g**

1 cauliflower (small), florets divided
1 pound (500 grams) broccoli
1 Romanesco cauliflower (small), florets divided
2 oranges (seedless), peeled & sliced thinly

Vinaigrette:
1 hot pepper (preferably fresh), chopped or sliced to preference
1 orange, zested & squeezed
1 tablespoon capers, packed in salt, unrinsed
4 anchovies
4 tablespoons olive oil (extra-virgin)
Salt & pepper to taste

1. Vinaigrette: You can either leave the ingredients whole or chop them finely, except for the hot pepper. In your vinaigrette container, add all the ingredients; shake to mix and set aside.
2. Peel the oranges using a knife or your hands; remove all the bitter white pith. Slice each orange crosswise into thin rounds. If using oranges that are not seedless, pick out the seeds.
3. Put the IP steamer basket in the inner pot and pour 1 cup water. Put all of the florets in the basket. Lock the lid and close the pressure valve. Set to LOW PRESSURE for 6 minutes. QPR when the timer beeps; unlock the lid and open.
4. Transfer the florets to a serving platter. Add the orange slices and mix. Shake the vinaigrette and pour over the top. Serve.

# SOUPS, STEWS, CHOWDERS, & CHILIES

## Carrot Soup

Servings|**4**    Prep. Time|**10 minutes**    Cook Time|**8 minutes**
**Nut. Content (per serving):** Cal|**323**    Fat|**26.4g**    Protein|**6.3g**    Carbs|**20g**

1 clove garlic, minced
1 teaspoon salt
1/2 onion (medium) diced
1/2 teaspoon pepper
15-ounce (canned) coconut milk
2 cups broth (vegetable)

8 carrots (large), peeled & cubed into 4-inch chunks
Bread (toasted), to serve
Coconut cream to serve
Parsley, chopped to serve

1. Set the IP to SAUTE. Once HOT, add the oil, garlic, and onion; sauté till the onion is soft. Press CANCEL. Add the pepper, salt, carrots, broth, and coconut milk; stir to mix well. Lock the lid and close the pressure valve. Set to HIGH PRESSURE for 8 minutes.
2. QPR when the timer beeps; unlock the lid and open. Stir the soup to mix well. Puree using a stick blender or in batches using a regular blender till smooth. Serve cold or hot drizzled with coconut cream, garnished with parsley and with toasted bread.

## Cream of Broccoli Soup

Servings|**6**    Prep. Time|**5 minutes**    Cook Time|**15 minutes**
**Nut. Content (per serving):** Cal|**163.6**    Fat|**4g**    Protein|**6.7g**    Carbs|**27.7g**

1 cup (250 milliliters) whole milk (or any nut milk of your choice)
1 pound (500 grams) broccoli stems & florets, divided & roughly chopped
1 tablespoon olive oil
1 teaspoon mustard (Dijon)

1 white onion, roughly chopped
2 garlic cloves, finely minced
2 teaspoons salt (remove if using salted stock)
3 potatoes (medium), roughly chopped
4 cups (1 liter) stock (vegetable)

1. Set the IP to SAUTE. Once HOT, add the olive oil and onion; cook till one side of the onion is slightly brown. Add the broccoli stems and trimmings, potato, and salt; stir to mix well. Add the stock. Heap the broccoli florets on top – DO NOT MIX.
2. Lock the lid and close the pressure valve. Set to HIGH PRESSURE for 5 minutes. QPR when the timer beeps; unlock the lid and open. Add the milk, garlic, and mustard; puree till smooth using an immersion blender. Serve.

## Baked Potato Loaded Soup

Servings|**4**    Prep. Time|**20 minutes**    Cook Time|**5 minutes**
**Nut. Content (per serving):** Cal|**0**    Fat|**0g**    Protein|**0g**    Carbs|**0g**

1 1/2 teaspoon salt
1 cup cheddar cheese (sharp), shredded
1/2 cup sour cream
1/2 onion (medium), diced
1/2 teaspoon flakes red pepper, crushed
1/2 teaspoon pepper

12 ounces bacon, crosswise sliced into bite-sized pieces
2 tablespoons chives (fresh), sliced
3 to 4 (white or red) medium potatoes, scrubbed & sliced into 2-inch chunks
4 cups broth (chicken)
Bread to serve

1. Set the IP to SAUTE. Once HOT, add the bacon; sauté for 5 minutes or till crisp. Press CANCEL. Transfer the bacon to a plate lined with paper towels using a slotted spoon.
2. Drain the bacon grease from the inner pot into a heatproof container by taking it out using a hot pod. Add the potatoes, onion, pepper, red pepper, salt, and broth; stir to mix well.
3. Lock the lid and close the pressure valve. Set to HIGH PRESSURE for 5 minutes. NPR for 10 minutes when the timer beeps and QPR; unlock the lid and open. Add the sour cream; stir to mix well. By one handful, add the cheese; stir till the cheese melts and well mixed. Divide between 4 bowls. Top each serving with bacon and the chives. Pair with bread.

## Tortilla Chicken Soup

Servings|**6**    Prep. Time|**5 minutes**    Cook Time|**8 minutes**
**Nut. Content (per serving):** Cal|**276**    Fat|**5g**    Protein|**25g**    Carbs|**32g**

1 1/2 cup corn (frozen)
1 can tomatoes (fire-roasted) chopped
1 pound chicken breast, sliced through the middle
1 tablespoon olive oil
1 teaspoon cumin (ground)
1 teaspoon paprika
15 ounces (canned) black beans, rinsed & drained
2 garlic cloves, chopped finely
2 teaspoon chili powder

2 teaspoon coriander (ground)
3/4 teaspoon salt
32 ounces broth (chicken, low sodium)

Add-ons (optional):
1 celery rib, chopped
1 carrot (medium), chopped

Garnish:
2 tablespoon cilantro, chopped
1 lime, juice only

1. Put all of the ingredients in the IP in no particular order; stir to mix well. Lock the lid and close the pressure valve. Set to HIGH PRESSURE for 8 minutes. NPR for 5 minutes when the timer beeps and QPR; unlock the lid and open. Remove the chicken to a slicing board; shred using 2 forks. Return the chicken to the pot. Add the cilantro and lime juice. Serve topped as preferred, such as tortilla chips, avocado, sour cream, cheese, etc.

# Firehouse Chili

Servings|**6**    Prep. Time|**15 minutes**    Cook Time|**23 minutes**
**Nut. Content (per serving):** Cal|**340**    Fat|**10.6g**    Protein|**31g**    Carbs|**32g**

1 medium bell pepper (green), stemmed, cored, &chopped (1 cups)
1 medium cloves garlic, peeled & minced (1 teaspoon)
1 pound ground beef (lean)
1 pounds tomatoes (Roma or plum), chopped (2 cups)
1 tablespoon olive, vegetable, corn, or canola oil
1 teaspoon cumin (ground)

1/2 cup broth (chicken)
1/2 cup tomato paste
1/2 tablespoon oregano (dried)
1/2 teaspoon coriander (ground)
1/2 teaspoon salt (table)
½ medium yellow onion chopped (1/2 cup)
1/8 cup regular chili powder
7 1/2-ounce beans (red kidney), drained & rinsed (1/2 & 1/3 cups)

1. Set the IP to SAUTE for 10 minutes. Add the oil; let heat for 1 to 2 minutes. Add the onion, bell pepper, and garlic; sauté for 5 minutes or till the onion is soft. Stir in the tomatoes; sauté for 2 minutes or till they start to soften, stirring occasionally. Stir in the salt, coriander, cumin, oregano, and chili powder till fragrant. Add the beans and the broth. Add the crumbled beef; stir to mix well.
2. Press CANCEL. Lock the lid and close the pressure valve. Set to HIGH PRESSURE for 8 minutes. QPR when the timer beeps; unlock the lid and open. Set the IP to SAUTÉ for 5 minutes.
3. Stir in the tomato paste; let come to a full simmer, stirring often. Stir for 2 to 3 minutes while simmering till thick. Press CANCEL. Remove the inner pot from the housing. Serve with dollops of yogurt (plain Greek) or sour cream.

# Ethiopian-Inspired Lentil Stew

Servings|**6**   Prep. Time|**10 minutes**   Cook Time|**10 minutes**
**Nut. Content (per serving):** Cal|**173**   Fat|**6g**   Protein|**8g**   Carbs|**21g**

1 1/2 cups water
1 cup lentils (red), rinsed 2 to 3 times
1 onion (large), chopped finely
1 tablespoon garlic & ginger crushed, 2 cloves garlic & 1/2-inch ginger, or 1/2 teaspoon ginger powder & 1/2 teaspoon garlic powder
1 tablespoon tomato paste
1 teaspoon salt, or as needed
3 tablespoons butter (unsalted) or ghee
Drizzle lime juice to garnish before serving

Spice mixture (substitute with 1 1/2 tablespoons Berbere Seasoning if available):
1 1/2 teaspoon coriander powder
1 teaspoon paprika (smoked)
1/2 teaspoon cumin (ground)
1/2 teaspoon garam masala
1/2 teaspoon turmeric powder
1/4 teaspoon black pepper (ground)
1/4 teaspoon cayenne pepper
Pinch cinnamon (ground)

1. Set the IP to SAUTE. After 1 minute, add the ghee/butter and onion; sauté for 30 seconds. Add your garlic and your ginger; fry for around 30 seconds. Add the tomato paste and spices (Berbere seasoning); stir to mix well. Add the lentils and water; stir to mix. Press CANCEL.
2. Lock the lid and close the pressure valve. Set to HIGH PRESSURE for 5 minutes. NPR when the timer beeps; unlock the lid and open. Adjust seasoning as needed. Serve drizzled with lime juice. Serve with lemon vinaigrette dressed garden salad or sourdough flatbread.

# Quinoa & Minestrone Soup

Servings | 6    Prep. Time | **10 minutes**    Cook Time | **3minutes**
**Nut. Content (per serving):** Cal | **167**    Fat | **9g**    Protein | **7g**    Carbs | **14g**

Pressure Cook:
1 can Beans (Northern) or preferred beans, rinsed & drained
1 cup (2 medium) carrots, chopped
1 cup (2 ribs) celery, chopped
1 teaspoon black pepper (ground)
1 teaspoon Paprika (smoked)
1 teaspoon salt adjust to preference
1 to 2 tablespoons Chili Paste (Sambal Oelek) or Sriracha, adjust to preference
1/4 cup quinoa or 1/2 cup elbow macaroni
2 tablespoons olive oil (extra-virgin)
2 teaspoons 21 Seasoning Salute or preferred Italian Seasoning blend

2 to 3 cloves garlic, chopped, or 1/2 teaspoon garlic powder
1/2 can of diced tomatoes or 3 tablespoons of tomato paste
32 ounces broth (vegetable, low-sodium)

After cooking:
2 tablespoon Parmesan cheese (grated), to garnish
2 cups spinach (baby), chopped

Add-on (optional):
2 links chicken sausage (pre-cooked), chopped, optional

1. Put all the pressure cooking ingredients in the IP; stir to mix well. Lock the lid and close the pressure valve. Set to HIGH PRESSURE for 3 to 4 minutes. NPR for 5 minutes when the timer beeps and QPR; unlock the lid and open. Stir in the optional sausage and the spinach. Serve garnished with cheese.

# Chicken & Corn Chowder

Servings | **6**     Prep. Time | **10 minutes**     Cook Time | **20 minutes**
**Nut. Content (per serving):** Cal | **380**     Fat | **17g**     Protein | **25g**     Carbs | **32g**

1 cup carrots, chopped, around 1 large
1 cup celery, chopped, around 1 to 2 ribs
1 cup potatoes (Yukon gold), chunked into
1/2-inch cubes
1 pound chicken breast tenders, halves, or
regular (boneless & skinless)
1/2 green pepper, sliced to the size of the
diced onion
1/2 onion (medium), diced
2  spring onion stalks, sliced, green and
white parts separated
2 cups half-&-half or milk (full-fat)
2 garlic cloves, chopped finely, or 1/4
teaspoon garlic powder
2 tablespoons butter (unsalted)
3 cups corn kernels (fresh, thawed, if
frozen)

3 cups stock (chicken or vegetable)
6 cremini mushrooms. Cleaned & sliced
Spring onions, chopped, to garnish

Spices:
1 1/4 teaspoon salt adjust to preference
1 teaspoon 21 seasoning salute (trader
Joe's) or preferred Italian spice blend
1 teaspoon black pepper (preferably fresh
ground)
1/4 teaspoon cayenne, optional
1/8 teaspoon nutmeg (ground)

Slurry mixture (optional):
3 to 4 tablespoons milk/water/broth
1 tablespoon cornstarch

1. Prepare all the veggies before cooking. Blend 1 cup half-&-half and 1 1/2 cups corn till well mixed.
2. Set the IP to SAUTE MORE mode. Once HOT, add the butter and melt. Add the mushrooms and potatoes; sauté for 30 seconds. Add the rest of the chopped veggies and white parts of the spring onion; sauté for 1 minute. Add the corn mixture.
3. Add the stock, all the spices, chicken, and remaining corn; stir to mix well. Lock the lid and close the pressure valve. Press CANCEL. Set to HIGH PRESSURE for 6 minutes. NPR for 10 to 15 minutes when the timer beeps and QPR; unlock the lid and open.
4. Set the IP to SAUTÉ. Transfer the chicken to a cutting board. The soup may look curdled, but do not worry; the blended corn just rose to the top. They will get blended. Add the rest of the half-&-half; stir to mix.
5. Optional step: Blend the chowder for a couple of seconds with a hand blender till thick. Alternatively, you can add the cornstarch slurry to the chowder while continuously stirring. Return the chicken in the pot; stir to mix. Serve garnished with spring onions.

## Chicken Chili

Servings|**5**    Prep. Time|**10 minutes**    Cook Time|**8 minutes**
**Nut. Content (per serving):** Cal|**340**    Fat|**11g**    Protein|**25g**    Carbs|**37g**

1 1/2 tablespoons vinegar (red wine)
1 1/3 ounces taco seasoning
1 pound ground chicken, beef, or turkey
1 tablespoon cocoa powder (unsweetened) optional, but recommended
1 tablespoon olive oil (light)
1 teaspoon sugar (brown)
1/2 cup onion, chopped (around 1/2 medium)
1/2 cup water
14 ounces (canned)  green chilies (diced)

14 ounces (canned) diced or crushed tomatoes
14 ounces (canned) pinto or kidney beans, rinsed & drained
2 cloves garlic, chopped finely

Garnishes & sides:
Cheddar cheese, shredded
Cornbread
Sour cream
Spring onions, chopped

1. Set the IP to SAUTE MORE mode. Add the oil, onion, and garlic; sauté for 30 seconds. Add the ground meat; sauté for 2 to 3 minutes, breaking the clumps using a wooden spoon. Add the beans, cocoa powder, green chilies, tomatoes, water, and taco seasoning; stir to mix well.
2. Cancel SAUTE. Lock the lid and close the pressure valve. Set to HIGH PRESSURE for 8 minutes. NPR for 10 minutes when the timer beeps and QPR; unlock the lid and open. Mash some of the beans to thicken the chilli using a wooden spoon. Set the IP to SAUTÉ; cook for 2 to 3 minutes. Serve garnished with preferred toppings and sides.

# Sweet Corn Chicken Soup

Servings|**4**   Prep. Time|**10 minutes**   Cook Time|**8 minutes**
**Nut. Content (per serving):** Cal|**85**   Fat|**02**   Protein|**8g**   Carbs|**6g**

Pressure Cook:
1 1/2 cups sweet corn (yellow), frozen or fresh
1 cup (about 2) carrots, chopped finely
1 tablespoon soy sauce
1 tablespoon vinegar (rice)
1/2 teaspoon black pepper
2 garlic cloves, chopped finely or grated
2 spring onions (white part)
2 teaspoons ginger (crushed), around 1-inch
3/4 teaspoon salt
4 cups stock or broth (chicken)
4 ounces chicken breast

Vinegar-chili garnish (optional):
3 tablespoon vinegar (rice)
1 jalapeno, thinly sliced

Creamed corn:
1 cup sweet corn (yellow), fresh, thawed if frozen
1/4 water or stock

After cooking:
1 egg, beaten
1/2 cup cabbage, shredded thinly
1/2 teaspoon sesame oil
2 spring onions (green part), sliced

Slurry (optional):
2 tablespoons water
2 teaspoons cornstarch

1. Creamed corn: Blend the water with the corn till a semi-smooth paste.
2. Pressure cook: Put all the ingredients in the pot. Add the creamed corn. Lock the lid and close the pressure valve. Set to HIGH PRESSURE for 8 minutes. NPR for 5 minutes when the timer beeps and QPR; unlock the lid and open.
3. Set the IP to SAUTE; adjust the seasoning as needed. Add the sesame oil and cabbage. While continuously stirring, add the beaten egg in the pot to cook the eggs into ribbons and to thicken the soup.
4. If you want a thicker soup, mix the slurry ingredients till smooth. Add to the pot; let come to a simmer. Turn off the SAUTE mode. Serve garnished with spring onions.
5. If using the optional garnish, put the ingredients in a small, microwavable bowl; microwave for 30 seconds and let cool.

# Super Tomato Soup

Servings|**4 - 6**   Prep. Time|**5 minutes**   Cook Time|**15 minutes**
**Nut. Content (per 6 servings):** Cal|**300.2**   Fat|**16.1g**   Protein|**6.4g**   Carbs|**37.6g**

1 carrot (medium), roughly chopped
1 onion (medium), roughly sliced
1 potato (medium), roughly diced
2 pinches black pepper
2 teaspoon salt
28 ounces (800 grams) canned tomatoes in their juice (high-quality, whole)
3 heaping tablespoon tomato paste or concentrate (2x or 3x strength)

3 heaping tablespoon tomatoes (sun-dried, rinsed if packed in oil, roughly chopped
4 cups or 1-liter water
4 tablespoons (60 grams) butter

Garnish:
Sour or fresh cream or yogurt (plain) adjust to preference

1. Set the IP to SAUTE. Once HOT, add the butter, carrot, onion, and pepper. Sauté for 5 minutes or till the onion start to soften, occasionally stirring. Add the sundried tomatoes, tomato paste, canned tomatoes, potatoes, salt, and water.
2. Lock the lid and close the pressure valve. Set to HIGH PRESSURE for 5 minutes. Cancel the KEEP WARM mode and unplug when the timer beeps. NPR for 10 to 15 minutes or till the indicator is down and QPR; unlock the lid and open.
3. Puree the contents using an immersion blender till smooth. Serve with cream or yogurt.

# Rosemary Veal Stew

Servings | **6**    Prep. Time | **10 minutes**    Cook Time | **25 minutes**
**Nut. Content (per serving):** Cal | **541**    Fat | **34g**    Protein | **46g**    Carbs | **14g**

1 cup wine (white)
1 tablespoon butter
1 tablespoon olive oil
2 carrots, chopped
2 celery stalks, chopped
2 sprigs rosemary (fresh), 1 chopped finely & 1 to garnish
2 tablespoons flour (all-purpose)

2 teaspoons salt, discard if using salted stock
3 pounds (1 1/2 kilograms) veal, chunked into 1-inch cubes
8 ounces (250 grams) shallots (around 15 small)
Stock (white veal) or water

1. Set the IP to SAUTE. Once HOT, add the oil, butter, and chopped rosemary. Mix in the celery, carrot, and shallot; sauté till the shallots are just beginning to turn soft.

2. Meanwhile, mix the veal with the flour, shaking off any excess – do not leave to much flour or the IP will scorch. Push your veggies to 1 side of your pot. Add the meat in the cleared part; cook till 2 sides are brown. Add the wine. Scrape the brown bits off using a wooden spoon or spatula; stir to mix well. Add just enough stock and water to almost cover the meat, but not submerged.

3. Lock the lid and close the pressure valve. Set to HIGH PRESSURE for 15 to 20 minutes. QPR gradually when the timer beeps; unlock the lid and open. Set the IP to SAUTE. Let come to a simmer; cook for 5 minutes or till the cooking juice is thick to preference. Serve on creamy polenta.

# Cream of Mushroom Soup

Servings|**4 - 6**    Prep. Time|**5 minutes**    Cook Time|**15 minutes**
**Nut. Content (per 6 servings):** Cal|**255.8**    Fat|**17.5g**    Protein|**3 1/2g**    Carbs|**22.1g**

1 1/2 pounds (750 grams) Portobello, white, or cremini mushrooms (fresh), 1 handful sliced finely & the remaining roughly chopped
1 1/2 teaspoons salt (sea), discard if using store-bought stock
1 celery stalk, roughly chopped
1 cup (250milliliters) cream (fresh)
1 ounce (30 grams) dried mushrooms (Shiitake Porcini, or Oyster), rinsed
1 red onion (medium), roughly chopped

1 tablespoon olive oil
1 teaspoon black pepper (fresh ground)
2 potatoes (large), peeled & roughly chopped (around 500 grams or 1 pound)
2 tablespoons red wine (tart dry, such as like Chianti)
4 cups (1 liter) stock (vegetable) (salt-free)

Optional:
1 teaspoon white truffle spread

1. Set the IP to SAUTE. Once HOT, add the olive oil and sliced thin mushrooms; sauté for around 5 minutes or till both sides are golden. Transfer to a plate; set aside.
2. Add the onions and celery; sauté till the onion is soft. Push the veggies to 1 side. Add enough roughly chopped mushrooms to the cleared side to cover the base, around 2 handfuls, and cook for 5 minutes or till lightly brown, stirring occasionally.
3. Add the wine. Scrape the brown bits off the pot; stir to mix well. Add the rest of the chopped mushrooms (not the sautéed sliced), potatoes, dried mushrooms, and salt; stir to mix well. Lock the lid and close the pressure valve. Set to HIGH PRESSURE for 7 minutes. QPR when the timer beeps; unlock the lid and open.
4. Add the cream, truffle, and pepper. Puree using an immersion blender till the mixture is smooth. Stir in the sautéed mushrooms, saving some to garnish. Serve.

# Potato Chili

Servings | **5 cups**     Prep. Time | **10 minutes**     Cook Time | **4 minutes**
**Nut. Content (per serving):** Cal | **165**     Fat | **6.3g**     Protein | **15.2g**     Carbs | **14.4g**

1 1/2 cups sweet potato, diced
1 1/2 teaspoon cumin
1 bay leaf (small)
1 large or 2 small cloves garlic, minced
1 teaspoon paprika (smoked)
1/2 cup water
1/2 of a 4-ounce can hot or mild green chilies (diced)
1/2 pound ground lean beef or turkey (97% lean)
1/2 sweet (small) or 1 yellow, diced (or yellow)
1/2 teaspoon Mexican or regular oregano
1/4 teaspoon pepper
1/4 teaspoon thyme (dried)
1/8 teaspoon chili powder (chipotle)

14-ounces (canned) diced tomatoes, with juice
14-ounces (canned) tomato sauce
15-ounces (canned) red kidney beans (drained & rinsed)
2 teaspoons chili powder
3/4 teaspoon kosher or 1/2 teaspoon salt (table)

Garnishes:
Avocado (fresh)
Cilantro leaves (fresh)
Corn Tortillas, sliced
Cotija or preferred Cheese
Tortilla Chips, crushed

1. Set the IP to SAUTE NORMAL mode. Once HOT, add the meat (add 2 teaspoons olive oil first if using turkey); cook till the meat is almost done. Add the onion; stir and cook till turning translucent. Add the garlic; stir for 1 minute or till fragrant. Add the pepper, salt, paprika, chipotle powder, thyme, oregano, cumin, chili powder, and green chilies; stir to mix well.
2. Add the tomatoes with the juices; stir to mix well. Add the tomato sauce, potatoes, kidney beans, water, and bay leaf; stir to mix. Let come to a simmer, occasionally stirring. Once simmering, stir one more time.
3. Lock the lid and close the pressure valve. Set to MANUAL HIGH PRESSURE for 5 minutes. NPR for 5 minutes when the timer beeps and QPR; unlock the lid and open. Stir to mix, removing the bay leaf. Serve with preferred garnish. This dish tastes even better when you let it sit for a while.
NOTES: Stay by the time at the start of pressure cooking. With chillies, the IP may start counting the time down even without coming to a pressure. If this occurs, and the lid is DOWN, open the pot, stir the contents well, scraping the bottom of your pot. Return the lid and reset the pressure valve. CANCEL and reset the timer. Stay till the pot reaches pressure.

# SIDE DISHES

## Cranberry Sauce

Servings | **14 ounces**     Prep. Time | **0 minutes**     Cook Time | **12 minutes**
**Nut. Content (per serving):** Cal | **50**     Fat | **0g**     Protein | **0g**     Carbs | **13g**

1/2 cup sugar
1/4 cup orange juice, honey, or agave syrup
12 ounces cranberries (fresh)

2 tablespoons water
Pinch salt
Zest of 1 orange (medium), optional

1. Turn ON the IP. Add the water then agave syrup. Add the salt and cranberries; stir to mix. Lock the lid and close the pressure valve. Set to HIGH PRESSURE for 1 minute. NPR for 7 minutes when the timer beeps and QPR; unlock the lid and open.
2. Set the IP to SAUTE. Add the sugar; stir and cook for 2 to 3 minutes or till the mixture is jam-like. Let cool for 10 minutes. Pour into glass jars.

## Sweet & Sour Pearl Onions

Servings | **4**     Prep. Time | **10 minutes**     Cook Time | **10 minutes**
**Nut. Content (per serving):** Cal | **62**     Fat | **0.11g**     Protein | **1.1g**     Carbs | **14.5g**

1 bay laurel leaf
Pinch salt
1 pound (500 grams) Cipolline
1 tablespoon flour (all-purpose)

1 tablespoon honey
1/2 cup (125 milliliters) water
3 to 4 tablespoons vinegar (balsamic)

1. Slice both ends of the onions off. Remove the first white layers. You can also try and peel off the paper-like thin skin. Put them in the IP. Add the water, bay leaf, and salt. Lock the lid and close the pressure valve. Set to LOW PRESSURE for 5 minutes. QPR when the timer beeps; unlock the lid and open.
2. While the onions are cooking, prepare the sauce. Put the vinegar, honey, and flour in a saucepan (small) set on the stove. Turn the heat/flame to very low. Quickly stir using a wooden spoon and keep stirring till the lumps are gone, around 30 seconds. Remove the heat immediately.
3. Once the onions are cooked, add the sauce in the pot; stir to mix well. Transfer the mixture to a serving platter. Serve. If desired, refrigerate the onions overnight before serving to intensify the flavor.

# Spiced Spinach & Mustard Greens

Servings|6    Prep. Time|**5 minutes**    Cook Time|**15 minutes**
**Nut. Content (per 1/2 cup):** Cal|**61**    Fat|**2g**    Protein|**2g**    Carbs|**8g**

Greens:
2 green chilies
4 cups spinach, stems removed & chopped

6 cups mustard greens, stems removed & chopped

Masala seasoning:
1 onion (medium), coarsely chopped
1 teaspoon cumin seeds
1 teaspoon garam masala
1 teaspoon salt adjust to preference
1/2 teaspoon chili powder (red), adjust to preference
1/2 teaspoon turmeric powder, optional

2 tablespoons cornflour or meal
2 tablespoons garlic & ginger paste, 1-inch ginger plus 6 cloves garlic, crushed/grated
2 teaspoons butter or ghee
2 to 3 teaspoons coriander powder
3/4 cup water

1.  Rinse the mustard greens and the spinach leaves 2 to 3 times to remove any dirt. Remove the stems off the mustard greens; roughly chop the leaves. Do the same process for the spinach leaves. Put the chopped greens and 2 green chilies in microwavable bowl; microwave for 2 minutes. Puree the greens to medium-fine texture adjust to preference with your hand blender.
2. Set the IP to SAUTE. Add the oil. Once heated, add the garlic & ginger paste and the cumin; sauté for 30 seconds. Add the onion; sauté for 30 seconds. Add the water, spices, and salt; stir to mix well. Cancel SAUTE. Lock the lid and close the pressure valve. Set to HIGH PRESSURE for 2 minutes. QPR when the timer beeps; unlock the lid and open.
3. Set the IP to SAUTE. Add the cornmeal; saute for 1 minute to cook it through. Add just a little meal if the mixture looks dry. Add the pureed greens; saute for 2 minutes to blend the flavors. Serve with cornmeal flatbread, naan, or corn tortillas.

# Garlic Cauliflower Potato Mash

Servings|4    Prep. Time|**5 minutes**    Cook Time|**15 minutes**
**Nut. Content (per serving):** Cal|**249.1**    Fat|**0.6g**    Protein|**7.5g**    Carbs|**55.9g**

1 1/2 cups water
1 garlic clove, minced
1/2 teaspoon salt

2 pounds (1 kilogram) potatoes (golden or white), cubed into 1-inch chunks
8 ounces (250 grams) cauliflower florets (fresh)

1. Put the potatoes and water in the IP; layer the potatoes evenly. Spread the cauliflower on top of the potatoes. Lock the lid and close the pressure valve. Set to HIGH PRESSURE for 5 minutes for fresh or for 10 minutes for frozen potatoes. QPR when the timer beeps; unlock the lid and open. Add the raw garlic and salt; mash and serve.

## Peperonata Side Dish or Sauce

Servings | **2**    Prep. Time | **5 minutes**    Cook Time | **15 minutes**
**Nut. Content (per serving):** Cal | **132**    Fat | **1.3g**    Protein | **5.5g**    Carbs | **29g**

1 bunch parsley or basil
1 green pepper, thinly sliced
1 red onion, sliced into thin strips
2 garlic cloves
2 red peppers, sliced into thin strips

2 ripe tomatoes (medium), or 14 1/2 ounces or 240 milliliters canned chopped tomatoes
2 yellow peppers, thinly sliced
Olive oil (fresh, unfiltered)
Salt & pepper

1. Rinse the peppers. Remove the stems and deseed. A few couple seeds are alright. Slice them into thin strips. Rinse the tomatoes. Chop them in the chopper till pulpy.
2. Set the IP to SAUTE. Once HOT, add the oil and onion; saute till the onions begin to soften. Add the peppers, 1 garlic with the skin on, and let cook for 5 minutes without stirring or till one side of the peppers are brown. Add the tomato puree as needed, pepper, and salt; stir to mix well.
3. Lock the lid and close the pressure valve quickly. Set to HIGH PRESSURE for 5 to 6 minutes. QPR when the timer beeps; unlock the lid and open. Remove the skin of the garlic. Using tongs, transfer the peppers to a serving dish. Add 1 pressed raw clove garlic, basil, and 1 swirl fresh olive oil. Mix and serve.
NOTES: You can leave out the tomato puree if the juices from the peppers reach a 1/4-inch level in the cooker. Otherwise, add tomato puree to reach the level.

## Baked Potatoes

Servings | **4**    Prep. Time | **5 minutes**    Cook Time | **25 minutes**
**Nut. Content (per serving):** Cal | **150**    Fat | **0g**    Protein | **6g**    Carbs | **39.2g**

2 pounds (1 kilogram) baking potatoes (medium) aka old or Idaho potatoes, well-scrubbed (around 6 pieces)

1 cup water

1. Pierce the potatoes a few times using the tip of a knife or a fork. Put them in the IP. Add the water. Set the oven to 450F to preheat it while the potatoes are cooking.
2. Lock the lid and close the pressure valve. Set to HIGH PRESSURE for 10 minutes. QPR when the timer beeps; unlock the lid and open. Carefully transfer the potatoes directly in the middle rack of the oven, making sure you do not remove too much of the skin; bake for 10 to 15 minutes. Remove the smallest potatoes; serve first. Turn off the oven. Let the larger potatoes finish cooking with the residual heat for around 5 to 10 minutes.

## Cabbage & Bacon Beer Braise

Servings|**4**    Prep. Time|**5 minutes**    Cook Time|**13 minutes**
**Nut. Content (per serving):** Cal|**284**    Fat|**20g**    Protein|**9.4g**    Carbs|**21g**

1 cup (250 milliliters) blonde beer or stock (vegetable)
1 medium head savoy cabbage (around 1 1/2 pounds or 750 grams), cut into strips

1 onion (medium), cut into strips
1 tablespoon butter
3 1/2 ounces (100 grams) smoked pancetta or bacon, cubed

1. Slice the cabbage into halves. Slice each half into strips. Wash the cabbage strips and dry them.
2. Set the IP to SAUTE. Once HOT, add the butter, onion, and pancetta/bacon; saute for 5 minutes or till the onion starts to soften. Add the cabbage and beer. Lock the lid and close the pressure valve. Set to HIGH PRESSURE for 3 minutes.
3. QPR when the timer beeps; unlock the lid and open. Immediately transfer the cabbage to a serving plate to stop cooking; mix and serve.

## Roman-Style Sautéed Fava Bean

Servings|**3**    Prep. Time|**10 minutes**    Cook Time|**15 minutes**
**Nut. Content (per serving):** Cal|**307**    Fat|**13g**    Protein|**14g**    Carbs|**42g**

1 teaspoon olive oil
1/2 cup wine (white)
2 to 3 sprigs parsley, chopped finely
3 pounds (1 1/2 kilograms) fava pods (fresh) in their pods, shelled

3/4 cup water
4 ounces (100 grams) bacon or smoked pancetta, diced
Pepper (fresh ground), to taste

1. Set the IP to SAUTE. Once HOT, add the oil and bacon/pancetta. Once starting to brown and crisp, add the wine to deglaze; scrape the brown bits off the pot using a spatula and mix. Cook till your wine is almost gone. Add the fava and water.
2. Lock the lid and close the pressure valve. Set to HIGH PRESSURE for 5 to 7 minutes. QPR when the timer beeps; unlock the lid and open. Season with pepper. Garnish with parsley. Serve warm or bring to temperature with preferred short pasta and topped with cheese (Pecorino Romano).

# Italian Rice Salad

Servings|4    Prep. Time|10 minutes    Cook Time|10 minutes
**Nut. Content (per serving):** Cal|479    Fat|24.7g    Protein|20g    Carbs|35g

Rice:
1 dash olive oil
Pinch salt

2 cups rice (Arborio, Ribe, or Roma)
4 cups water

Salad:
1 bunch basil, chopped
1 cup olives (green or black), chopped
1 mozzarella ball, cubed (omit if using tuna)
2 tomatoes (fresh), chopped
3 eggs (hard-boiled), 2 chopped & 1 wedged
to decorate

3 tablespoons capers, packed in vinegar
(jarred artichokes or pickles)
4 ounces ham, diced, any leftover meat, or
tuna fish
Olive oil

1. Put the rice, olive oil, salt, and water in the IP; stir to mix. Prepare a strainer (rice or fine mesh) in the sink. Lock the lid and close the pressure valve. Set to HIGH PRESSURE for 4 minutes. QPR gradually when the timer beeps; unlock the lid and open.
2. Immediately strain the rice in the sink. Run cold water on it to stop cooking and rinse any starch. Transfer to a mixing bowl. Add the rest of the salad ingredients. Serve at room temperature or chilled.

# Coconut Beet Stir Fry

Servings|4    Prep. Time|10 minutes    Cook Time|10 minutes
**Nut. Content (per serving):** Cal|6    Fat|4g    Protein|2g    Carbs|14g

1 teaspoon coriander powder
1 teaspoon lime juice (fresh)
1 teaspoon mustard seeds (dark)
1 teaspoon salt
1/2 teaspoon turmeric powder
1/4 cup coconut flakes (unsweetened)

1/4 teaspoon cayenne, optional
2 teaspoons coconut oil olive oil (light) or
ghee
4 cups beets, peeled & chopped, pulsed 5 to
6 times in your food processor

1.  Set the IP to SAUTE MORE mode. Once HOT, add the mustard seeds; let them splutter and sizzle. Add green chilies and curry leaves at this point if using. Add the beets; sauté for 1 minute. Add the spices and grated coconut; stir to mix well. Cover with the IP glass lid or similar; cook for 2 minutes. Remove the lid; sauté for 1 minute. Adjust seasoning as needed. Drizzle with lime juice.

# CAKES & SWEETS

## Fresh Strawberry Topped Angel Food Cake

Servings | **4**    Prep. Time | **15 minutes**    Cook Time | **4 minutes**
**Nut. Content (per serving):** Cal | **185**    Fat | **0.5g**    Protein | **7g**    Carbs | **37.4g**

1 teaspoon cream of tartar
1 teaspoon Vanilla
1/2 cup flour (all-purpose), finely sifted or cake flour
1/4 cup sugar (powdered)

3/4 cup sugar
6 egg whites
Pinch salt
Strawberries (fresh), sliced & whipped cream to serve

1. In a bowl (small), whisk the salt, sugar, and flour till incorporated. In a different bowl (large), whisk the egg whites till foamy with a mixer (handheld) using medium speed.
2. Add the cream of tartar, increase the mixer to high and whip till soft peaks appear. Add the vanilla, whisk till mixed. Turn off your mixer. Carefully fold the flour mixture into the egg white mixture till mixed – do not overmix.
3. Divide the batter between 2 pieces ungreased springform pans (ungreased), filling them to the top. Loosely cover with foil, making room for the expansion. Put the IP trivet in the inner pot and pour 3/4 cup water. Put 1 pan on the steam rack.
3. Lock the lid and close the pressure valve. Set to HIGH PRESSURE for 25 minutes. QPR when the timer beeps; unlock the lid and open carefully to prevent any condensation from falling on the cake. Remove the pans from the pot. Repeat the pressure cooking process with the second cake.
4. Let the cakes cool for 1 hour. Run a knife around each cake to loosen them from the pan. Unlock the sides and run a knife under the cake to release from the bottom of the pan. Serve each with 1 dollop cream (whipped) and strawberries if desired.
NOTES: You can stack the pans to cook the cakes, but they will not be as fluffy and light as cooking them separately.

# 15-Minute Chocolate Lava Cake

Servings|**4**    Prep. Time|**5 minutes**    Cook Time|**15 minutes**
**Nut. Content (per serving):** Cal|**281**    Fat|**19g**    Protein|**3g**    Carbs|**24g**

1 egg

1 egg yolk

1/2 teaspoon vanilla extract

2 ounces chocolate chips (semi-sweet, Ghirardelli)

3 tablespoons flour (all-purpose)

4 tablespoons (1/2 stick) butter,

6 tablespoons confectioners' sugar, use 1/2 cup for a sweeter cake

Pinch salt

Serving suggestions:

Powdered sugar, to dust the top

Salted caramel or vanilla ice-cream

1. Microwave the chocolate and the butter together for 30 to 60 seconds. Mix well using a whisk. Sift in the sugar; whisk again to mix. Add the egg and egg yolk, salt, and vanilla; whisk well. Sift in the flour; whisk till mixed.

2. Pour the batter into 4-ounce ramekins or cupcake molds, leaving a 1/4-inch clear space at the top. Put the IP trivet in the inner pot and pour 1 cup water. Put the molds on the trivet. Lock the lid and close the pressure valve. Set to HIGH PRESSURE for 7 minutes, 6 minutes for a gooier center, or for 9 minutes for a cake-like center.  QPR when the timer beeps; unlock the lid and open. Remove the cakes from the pot. Let cool for 2 minutes. Invert onto serving plates. Dust with sugar. Serve warm or top with ice cream.

# Mulled Wine

Servings|**4**    Prep. Time|**10 minutes**    Cook Time|**10 minutes**
**Nut. Content (per serving):** Cal|**244**    Fat|**0g**    Protein|**0g**    Carbs|**20g**

1 1/2 ounces Grand Marnier or Rum, optional

1 cinnamon stick

1 star anise

1/2 orange (medium)

1/4 cup sugar

10 cloves

3/4 cup water

750 milliliters (1 bottle) wine (red), such as cabernet sauvignon

1. Peel the orange; save the peel. Pierce the cloves into 1 or more of the orange peels; set aside. Extract the juice from the orange; set aside. If desired, strain the juice to remove the fibers.

2. Set the IP to SAUTE MORE mode. Add the water and sugar; let come to a boil. Stir to dissolve the sugar. Set the IP to SAUTE LESS mode. Add the orange juice, peels, orange peels with cloves, star anise, and cinnamon; simmer for 2 minutes. 3. Add the wine; let come to a steam, not boil. Press CANCEL. Set to KEEP WARM mode.

## Skinny Cheesecake

Servings | **6**  Prep. Time | **40 minutes**  Cook Time | **35 minutes**
**Nut. Content (per serving):** Cal | **267**  Fat | **19g**  Protein | **4g**  Carbs | **19g**

Crust:
1 teaspoon sugar (brown)
2 tablespoons butter (unsalted), melted
5 crackers (honey graham)

Cheesecake batter:
1 egg (large)
1/2 teaspoon vanilla extract
1/4 cup sugar
2 tablespoons sour cream
8 ounces cream cheese (Kraft Philadelphia), softened
Zest of 1 lime, optional, but recommended

1. In your food processor, grind the crackers finely. Mix the butter, sugar (brown), and crackers till well incorporated. Transfer the mixture to 7-inch nonstick pan, spread evenly on the bottom and slightly up the sides. Press down on the crust firmly to set it in the pan. Freeze for 20 minutes.

2. With your hand mixer or food processor, whip/blend the cream cheese for 30 seconds using LOW speed. Add the zest, vanilla, and sugar; blend for 30 seconds. Add the sour cream; blend for 30 seconds. Add the egg; blend for 15 to 20 seconds.

3. Remove the crust from the freezer. Pour the batter in. Gently wiggle the pan to make the bubbles rise to the top. Run a fork or an icing spatula through the batter to remove the air bubbles. Tightly cover the pan with a paper towel, making sure it does not stick to the cake, and then with foil to prevent moisture from getting in the cake.

4. Put the IP trivet in the inner pot and pour 1 cup water. Put the pan on the trivet. Lock the lid and close the pressure valve. Set to HIGH PRESSURE for 35 minutes. NPR for 17 to 18 minutes when the timer beeps and QPR; unlock the lid and open. If the cake is still jelly like

5. Carefully remove the pan from the pot. Remove the foil and parchment paper (if the cake is still jelly-like, pressure cook for 4 to 5 minutes more); let cool for 15 minutes. Using a knife or spatula, run around the cake to release it from the pan. Loosely cover the pan. Refrigerate for 8 to 10 hours. Unlock the pan and lift the base. Slide the cake in a serving platter. Serve as is or top with whipped cream, fresh berries, or any preferred topping.

# Indian Rice Pudding

Servings | **6**     Prep. Time | **5 minutes**     Cook Time | **35 minutes**
**Nut. Content (per serving):** Cal | **449**     Fat | **9g**     Protein | **14g**     Carbs | **76g**

1/2 cup rice (basmati or any white rice)
1/2 cup sugar adjust to preference
1/2 teaspoon ground cardamom, addition after cooking
1/3 cup chopped nuts (assorted, such as cashews, slivered almonds, or pistachios), omit for –nut-free
1/4 cup water
4 cups milk (2%, whole, unsweetened regular almond milk, or coconut milk

Optional ingredients (addition before cooking):
1 tablespoon flaked coconut (unsweetened)
1 tablespoon raisins
1/2 teaspoon saffron

Latin-American version:
1 teaspoon vanilla extract
1/2 cup rice (jasmine), rinsed 2 to 3 times
1/2 cup sugar adjust to preference
1/2 teaspoon cinnamon (ground) or 1 stick cinnamon
1/4 cup water
4 cups milk (2% or whole)

1. Rinse the rice 2 to 3 times or till the water runs clear. Soak in water while preparing the rest of the ingredients. Drain before using.
2. Set the IP to SAUTE. Add 1/4 cup water and the milk. Add the rice, nuts, and sugar; lightly stir. Press CANCEL. Set to PORRIDGE for 20 minutes. NPR for 15 minutes when the timer beeps and QPR; unlock the lid and open.
3. Mash the rice using a potato masher to make the pudding creamy. Add the cardamom and stir. Serve warm or cold.

## Mulled Cider

Servings | **6**    Prep. Time | **10 minutes**    Cook Time | **20 minutes**
**Nut. Content (per serving):** Cal | **236**    Fat | **0g**    Protein | **0g**    Carbs | **62g**

10 cloves (whole), adjust to preference
1-inch ginger, sliced
2 apples (Granny Smith), cored & sliced
3 cinnamon sticks

3/4 cup sugar (brown), adjust to preference
5 to 6 cups water
6 apples (Gala or Pink Lady), cored & sliced

1. Wrap the cinnamon and cloves in a cheesecloth securely. Core the apples and then slice them into 1/4-inch pieces. Turn ON the IP. Add all the ingredients in the pot; stir to mix well. Lock the lid and close the pressure valve. Set to HIGH PRESSURE for 15 minutes. NPR for 15 minutes when the timer beeps and QPR; unlock the lid and open.
2. Break down the apples using a spatula or mash them fully with a potato masher. Strain the mixture through a sieve set over a separate bowl. Push down on the pulp with a spatula. Once strained, strain again, lightly stirring to hold back the pulp. Save the pulp to use for pancakes or apple cakes.

## Fudgy Carrot Pudding

Servings | **8**    Prep. Time | **10 minutes**    Cook Time | **25 minutes**
**Nut. Content (per serving):** Cal | **301**    Fat | **11g**    Protein | **10g**    Carbs | **41g**

1 1/4 cups milk powder (nonfat)
1 cup milk, heated in the microwave for 2 minutes (2%, whole, or fat-free)
1 tablespoon almonds, chopped, to garnish, optional
1/2 teaspoon cardamom powder (green), or around 6 pods, deseeded & crushed

1/2 teaspoon saffron, optional
1/4 cup almonds & cashews, chopped
3/4 cup sugar
4 tablespoon ghee (unsalted) or butter
6 cups (10 to 12 medium or 5 to 6 large) carrots, grated

1. Prepare the ingredients before cooking. Set the IP to SAUTE. Once HOT, add the cooking fat, carrots, and nuts; saute for 2 to 3 minutes. Add the sugar, saffron, warm milk, and stir to mix well.
2. Lock the lid and close the pressure valve. Set to HIGH PRESSURE for 5 minutes. QPR when the timer beeps; unlock the lid and open. Set the IP to SAUTÉ. Add the milk powder; stir to mix. Cook for 10 to 15 minutes or till the liquid is gone. Add the cardamom powder. Garnish with the almonds. Serve.

# Salted Caramel Lava Cakes

Servings|**4**    Prep. Time|**10 minutes**    Cook Time|**10 minutes**
**Nut. Content (per serving):** Cal|**292**    Fat|**19g**    Protein|**3g**    Carbs|**26g**

1/2 stick (2 ounces or 4 tablespoons) butter, softened
2 ounces Chocolate Chips (semi-sweet, Ghirardelli)
6 tablespoons (powdered sugar) confectioners' sugar
1 egg
1 egg yolk
1/2 teaspoon vanilla extract

Pinch salt
3 tablespoons flour (all-purpose)
2 teaspoons salted caramel sauce

Serving suggestions:
Coarse salt (sea), optional
Powdered sugar, to dust the top
Toffee flavor or salted caramel ice cream

1. Microwave the chocolate and butter for around 30 to 60 seconds. Whisk till well mixed. Sift in the confectioner's sugar; whisk again. Add the salt, vanilla, and eggs; whisk well. Sift in the flour; whisk till mixed. Grease 4 ounces ramekins or silicone cupcake molds. Follow any of the options for assembling the cake.
2. Option 1: Pour caramel sauce in the bottom of the mold. Pour the batter on top, leaving a 1/4-inch clearance at the top. The caramel sauce will melt all over your lava cake when you invert it.
3. Option 2: Pour the battle in the molds, filling them half full. Pour 1 teaspoon or so of caramel sauce in the center. Pour the batter on top of the sauce, leaving a 1/4-inch clearance at the top. The caramel will ooze out with the chocolate lava from the cake.
4. Put the IP trivet in the inner pot and pour 1 cup water. Put the molds on the trivet. Lock the lid and close the pressure valve. Set to HIGH PRESSURE for 7 minutes or for 6 minutes for a gooier center. For a cake-like center, set the time for 8 to 9 minutes. QPR when the timer beeps; unlock the lid and open.
5. Remove the molds from the pot; let cool for 1 minute. Invert onto serving platters. Dust with sugar if desired. Serve with a scoop of ice cream. Serve.

## Carrot Fudge

Servings | **24**    Prep. Time | **10 minutes**    Cook Time | **25 minutes**
**Nut. Content (per serving):** Cal | **81**    Fat | **4g**    Protein | **2g**    Carbs | **9g**

1/2 cup almond meal or flour
1/2 cup milk powder (nonfat)
1/2 cup sugar
1/2 teaspoon cardamom powder (green), around 6 pods, deseeded & crushed
1/4 cup almonds & cashews, chopped

2 tablespoons almonds & cashews, chopped, to garnish
3 tablespoon butter or ghee (unsalted)
3/4 cup milk, microwave for 1 minute (2%, whole, or almond)
4 cups (around 7 to 9 medium or 4 to 5 large) carrots, grated

1. Prepare the ingredients before starting. Set the IP to SAUTE. Once HOT, add the ghee/butter, carrots, and chopped nuts; saute for 2 to 3 minutes. Add the warm milk and the sugar; stir to mix well. Lock the lid and close the pressure valve. Set to HIGH PRESSURE for 5 minutes. QPR when the timer beeps; unlock the lid and open.
2. Set the IP to SAUTE. Add the almond flour/meal and milk powder; stir to mix. Cook the liquid off; stir often for a couple of minutes initially, then every 30 seconds or so – this process will take about 8 to 10 minutes.
3. Add the cardamom powder; stir to mix. Transfer the mixture to a pan lined with parchment paper; spread evenly using a spatula or back of a spoon and smooth the top. Garnish with chopped nuts; press them gently into the fudge. Cover the pan and refrigerate for 30 minutes to 1 hour. Once set, slice into pieces. Serve with tea.

## Dulce De Leche Caramel

Servings | **28**    Prep. Time | **2 minutes**    Cook Time | **40 minutes**
**Nut. Content (per serving):** Cal | **45**    Fat | **1g**    Protein | **1g**    Carbs | **7g**

14 ounces (canned) condensed milk (sweetened)
6 cups water

1.  Pour the milk in a canning jar; cover the jar with aluminum foil tightly. Put the IP trivet in the inner pot. Add enough water to reach 1/2 inch below the top of the jar. Lock the lid and close the pressure valve. Set to HIGH PRESSURE for 40 minutes or 45 minutes for a light golden brown color. QPR when the timer beeps; unlock the lid and open.
2. Carefully remove the jar using a pot holder or kitchen towel from the hot pot. Remove the foil. The milk will look bit curdled. Stir for 30 seconds using a spatula or spoon till smooth. Keep refrigerated.

## Almond Saffron Pudding

Servings | **4**    Prep. Time | **20 minutes**    Cook Time | **30 minutes**
**Nut. Content (per serving):** Cal | **422**    Fat | **24g**    Protein | **9g**    Carbs | **47g**

1 cup almond meal or flour
1 tablespoon butter (unsalted) or ghee
1/2 cup water
1/2 teaspoon cardamom powder (around 5 to 6 cardamom pods, peeled & crushed)
1/2 teaspoon saffron

3/4 cup milk (almond milk, ore preferred dairy-free)
3/4 cup sugar (adjust to preference)
4 tablespoons almonds (slivered), save 1 tablespoon as a garnish

1. Set the IP to SAUTE. Add the butter or ghee. Once heated, add the almond and almond flour; saute for 3 to 4 minutes. Meanwhile, heat the mixed saffron and milk for 3 minutes in the microwave or in the stove top. Add the sugar to the almond mixture in the IP; stir to mix well. Add the milk mixture into the pot, whisking continuously as you pour it in.
2. Cancel SAUTE. Lock the lid and close the pressure valve. Set to HIGH PRESSURE for 4 minutes. QPR when the timer beeps; unlock the lid and open. Set the IP to SAUTE. Simmer the mixture for around 3 minutes or till the texture is pudding-like, stirring occasionally. The mixture will thicken as it cools. Garnish with the reserved almonds; serve warm.

## 2-Ingredient Plum Jam

Servings | **5 (8-ounce jars)**    Prep. Time | **15 minutes**    Cook Time | **45 minutes**
**Nut. Content (per 1 tbsp.):** Cal | **57**    Fat | **0g**    Protein | **0g**    Carbs | **14g**

10 cups plums, washed & pitted, chopped
5 to 6 1/2 cups sugar, adjust to preference

1. Put the plums and sugar in the IP. Set the pot to SAUTE. Let sit for 2 to 3 minutes, stirring once between, to help release enough juice for pressure cooking. Cancel SAUTE. Lock the lid and close the pressure valve. Set to MANUAL HIGH PRESSURE for 1 minute. NPR for 10 minutes when the timer beeps and QPR; unlock the lid and open.
2. Set the IP to SAUTE MORE mode. Cook for 20 to 30 minutes or till the jam is thick and spreadable, stirring occasionally. Take note that it will thicken more as it cools down. Let cool down completely before transferring to jars.

## Fudgy Brownies

Servings|**8**    Prep. Time|**5 minutes**    Cook Time|**40 minutes**
**Nut. Content (per serving):** Cal|**110**    Fat|**1g**    Protein|**1g**    Carbs|**25g**

2 eggs (large), bring to room temperature
1 stick butter, bring to room temperature
1 Brownie mix

1. Put the butter in a microwavable bowl (large); microwave for 20-second bursts till melted uniformly. Add the eggs in the bowl, whisk till well blended. Add the brownie mix; fold with a spatula – do not overmix. Keep folding till just mixed.
2. Grease an ovenproof baking pan. Line with parchment paper. Add the batter and spread to an even layer. Loosely cover with foil.
3. Put the IP trivet in the inner pot and pour 1 cup water. Put the pan on the trivet. Set to HIGH PRESSURE for 40 minutes. NPR for 10 minutes when the timer beeps and QPR; unlock the lid and open.
4. Carefully remove the pan from the pot. Run a plastic knife around the edges of the brownie. Release the lock and remove the ring. Let cool for 10 minutes before slicing.

## Tricky Carrots

Servings|**0**    Prep. Time|**5 minutes**    Cook Time|**10 minutes**
**Nut. Content (per serving):** Cal|**209**    Fat|**3.1g**    Protein|**4.1g**    Carbs|**45g**

1 tablespoon butter
1 tablespoon maple syrup
1/4 cup raisins

2 pounds or 1 kilogram carrots, peeled & diagonally sliced thickly
Pepper (fresh cracked) to taste

1. Wash the carrots. Peel them and then slice diagonally into thick pieces. Put them in the IP. Add the raisins and 1 cup water. Lock the lid and close the pressure valve. Set to LOW PRESSURE for 3 to 4 minutes. QPR when the timer beeps; unlock the lid and open.
2. Strain the carrots. Immediately add the butter to the still warm cooker and melt. Add the maple syrup. Stir to mix well. Add the strained carrots; carefully coat with the butter mixture. Serve warm sprinkle with pepper.

# Mango Cheesecake

Servings|**8**    Prep. Time|**10 minutes**    Cook Time|**30 minutes**
**Nut. Content (per serving):** Cal|**272**    Fat|**18g**    Protein|**4g**    Carbs|**23g**

Crust:
1/2 teaspoon cardamom (ground) or 6 to 8 pods
2 tablespoon brown or regular sugar
2 tablespoon butter, melted
3/4 cup pistachio, shelled

Topping:
1/4 cup confectioners' or powdered sugar
1/2 cup mango puree

Filling:
1 egg
1 tablespoon cornstarch
1/3 cup sugar (cane)
1/4 cup mango puree
8 ounces cream cheese
8 to 10 saffron strands, soaked in 1 tablespoon warm water
Pinch salt

1. Crust: Pulse the cardamom and pistachio in a food processor (small) till medium-fine or ground to preferred texture, around 8 to 10 pulses. Mix the pistachio mixture with the butter and sugar.
2. Line the bottom of a spring-form pan with a round piece of parchment paper. Pour the crust in the pan; press down on the bottom and slightly up the sides firmly. Refrigerate the crust till firm.
3. Filling: In a bowl (large) whisk the cream cheese using low speed for 45 seconds or till fluffy. Gradually mix in the saffron water (without strands), mango pulp, and sugar; blend for 30 to 45 seconds. Add the egg; blend for 30 to 40 seconds or till mixed. Pour the mixture into the prepared crust. Evenly spread the filling using a spatula or spoon. Break any bubbles in the filling using a fork or knife. Cover the pan with foil.
4. Put the IP trivet in the inner pot and pour 1 cup water. Put the pan on the trivet. Lock the lid and close the pressure valve. Set to HIGH PRESSURE for 30 minutes. NPR for 20 minutes when the timer beeps and QPR; unlock the lid and open.
5. Remove the pan from the pot. Remove the foil; let rest on the counter for 30 minutes. Release the cheesecake from the pan by running a spatula or butter knife around the cake edges. Carefully unlock the pan. Remove the ring; let cool down for 1 hour more.
6. Topping (optional, but highly recommended): Whisk the sugar and puree till mixed well. Pour over the cheesecake; spread using a spatula to an even layer. Chill in the fridge for a minimum of 8 hours till overnight. Serve.

# Hazelnut Chocolate Topped Limoncello Cheesecake

Servings | **8**    Prep. Time | **5 minutes**    Cook Time | **15 minutes**
**Nut. Content (per serving):** Cal | **267**    Fat | **19g**    Protein | **7.4g**    Carbs | **17g**

1 hazelnut chocolate bar
1 tablespoon vanilla extract or 1 envelope vanillin
1/3 cup (80 grams) sugar
1/4 cup (60 milliliters) Limoncello liqueur or lemon juice
2 eggs (large), bring to room temperature, beaten
2 tablespoons (30 grams) butter (unsalted), half softened, half melted

2 tablespoons grated lemon zest
4 ounces (125 grams) Biscotti cookies  or known as Cantucci in Italy
6 ounces (170 grams) ricotta, drained, bring to room temperature
8 ounces (225 grams) cream cheese, bring to room temperature

Materials (use any of the following):
1 piece 7-inch heatproof dish
2 pieces 1/2-liter jars

4 pieces 1/4-liter jars

1. Let the recipes come to room temperature 1 hour before making the recipe. Put the IP trivet in the inner pot and pour 2 cups water. Rub the bottom and the edges of your preferred cake container with the softened butter; set aside.
2. Melt the rest of the butter in a pan (small). Pulverize the cookies in a food chopper. Add the melted butter, blend to mix. Press the crumbs to the bottom of the cake container using the back of a spoon or your fingers into a 1/4-inch thick layer, nothing thicker. Refrigerate the container to firm the crust before continuing.
3. Put the ricotta in a mixing bowl. Break and mix using a hand blender or a fork by stirring vigorously. Add the sugar and cream cheese. Gradually add the vanilla, limoncello, and lemon zest. Once mixed, add the beaten eggs. The texture should be a super runny pancake batter texture.
4. Take out the cake container from the fridge. Carefully pour the cheese mixture over the crust using a soup ladle. Use a foil to cover the container tightly and put on the trivet.
5. Lock the lid and close the pressure valve. Set to HIGH PRESSURE for 15 to 20 minutes. NPR for 10 minutes when the timer beeps and QPR; unlock the lid and open. Carefully transfer the container to a cooling rack, raised platform, or trivet. Uncover; let sit for around 1 hour to cool. Refrigerate and chill for at least 4 hours before serving. Make splinters from the chocolate bar using a vegetable peeler. Wipe the condensation from the cake container. Sprinkle with the chocolate splinters.

## Chocolate Fondue

Servings|**2 -4**    Prep. Time|**1 minute** Cook Time|**10 minutes**
**Nut. Content (per 4 servings):** Cal|**216**    Fat|**20.3g**    Protein|**1.8g**    Carbs|**11.7g**

3 1/2 ounces (100 grams) cream (fresh) or coconut milk (unsweetened)
3 1/2 ounces (100 grams) 70-85% dark chocolate

1 teaspoon sugar, optional
1 teaspoon amaretto liquor, optional

1. Put the IP trivet in the inner pot and pour 2 cups water. In a small heatproof container (ceramic), such as a mug, ramekin, or fondue pot (small), add the chocolate. Add the same amount of cream, then the optional liquor and sugar if using, as well as any spices or aromatics you prefer.
2. Put the container on the trivet. Lock the lid and close the pressure valve. Set to HIGH PRESSURE for 2 minutes. QPR when the timer beeps; unlock the lid and open carefully to prevent any moisture to fall in the container. Remove the container from the pot using tongs or gloved hand.
3. Stir the contents vigorously for 1 minute using a fork; keep at it until the mixture is smooth. Serve right away or transfer to a fondue stand set to medium heat/flame. Serve with bite-sized fresh fruits, long, small cookies, or bread cubes.

## Chocolate Lava Cake in a Mug

Servings|**1**    Prep. Time|**5 minutes**    Cook Time|**10 minutes**
**Nut. Content (per serving):** Cal|**625.9**    Fat|**33 1/2g**    Protein|**12.1g**    Carbs|**77.9g**

1 egg (medium)
Pinch salt
1/2 teaspoon baking powder
2 cups (500 milliliters) water
2 tablespoons (20 grams) cocoa powder (unsweetened)

2 tablespoons (20 grams) olive oil
2 tablespoons (28 grams) preferred milk
4 tablespoons (45 grams) flour (all-purpose)
4 tablespoons (70 grams) granulated sugar

1. Put the IP trivet in the inner pot and pour 2 cups water; set aside. Rub the insides of the mug with a couple drops of oil; set aside.
2. In a bowl (small), mix the sugar and egg till the egg is fully whisked. Add the baking powder, salt, oil, milk, cocoa powder, and flour; mix well. Pour the mixture into the mug. Put the mug on the trivet.
3. Lock the lid and close the pressure valve. Set to HIGH PRESSURE for 10 minutes. QPR when the timer beeps; unlock the lid and open. Carefully remove the mug from the pot; serve.

# Lemon Peel Candies

Servings | **80-100 strips**    Prep. Time | **20 minutes**    Cook Time | **30 minutes**
**Nut. Content (per 2 strips):** Cal | **6.2**    Fat | **0g**    Protein | **0g**    Carbs | **1.7g**

5 cups (1 1/4 liters) water, divided
2 1/4 cups (450 grams) sugar (granulated white), divided

1 pound (500 grams) lemons (organic), around 5 lemons

1. Wash the lemons very well; use a scrubby sponge to clean the surface. Slice each lengthwise into halves and juice; reserve the juice for other uses. Slice the nubs off the t the tip and then slice each half into quarters.
2. Hold each peel flat on a slicing board, slice or peel out the pulp. Use a melon-baller to start peeling the pulp at the tip, then when you have enough to grab, use your fingers to peel the rest from the pulp. Slice each de-pulped peel into thin strips, around as thick as it is wide.
3. Put the peels in the IP. Add 4 cups water. Lock the lid and close the pressure valve. Set to HIGH PRESSURE for 3 minutes. QPR gradually when the timer beeps; unlock the lid and open. Strain the peel and rinse well. Discard the cooking water. Rinse the insert.
4. Put 1 cup water and 2 cups sugar in the IP. Add the lemon strips. Set the IP to SAUTE for 5 minutes. Cook uncovered for 5 minutes or till all the sugar is melted. Lock the lid and close the pressure valve. Set to HIGH PRESSURE for 10 minutes. Cancel the KEEP WARM mode and unplug when the timer beeps. NPR for 10 to 15 minutes or till the indicator is down and QPR; unlock the lid and open.
5. Strain the peels; save the delicate syrup for other use. Spread the peels on a parchment paper or cutting board; let cool for 15 minutes or more. Gently toss 4 to 5 peels in a plate (small) of sugar and coat. Shake off excess and put them on a sheet pan or fresh parchment paper. Refrigerate the peels and let stand for 4 hours uncovered or till completely dry – overnight is best.
6. Transfer the strips to a glass jar with seal. Store in a dry, cool place for 6 to 8 weeks or keep refrigerated for up to 6 months. Keep refrigerated if you live in a very humid area.
NOTES: Skip coating the peels with sugar if using them for baking desserts. They will be very sticky so just roll them in parchment paper before storing in a glass jar.

## Baked Apples

Servings|**6**    Prep. Time|**5 minutes**    Cook Time|**20 minutes**
**Nut. Content (per serving):** Cal|**188.7**    Fat|**0.3g**    Protein|**0.6g**    Carbs|**41.9g**

1 cup (250 milliliters) red wine
1 teaspoon cinnamon powder
1/2 cup (100 grams) sugar (raw demerara)

1/4 cup (30 grams) raisins
6 apples (fresh, with the green, flexible stem still attached), cored

1. Put the apples in the IP. Add the wine, cinnamon powder, sugar, and raisins. Lock the lid and close the pressure valve. Set to HIGH PRESSURE for 10 minutes. Cancel the KEEP WARM mode and unplug when the timer beeps. NPR for 10 to 15 minutes or till the indicator is down and QPR; unlock the lid and open. Scoop each apple into small serving bowls. Pour a generous amount of cooking liquid into each bowl. Serve.

## Ginger Peach Chutney

Servings|**16 ounces**    Prep. Time|**10 minutes**    Cook Time|**40 minutes**
**Nut. Content (per serving):** Cal|**64**    Fat|**0g**    Protein|**0g**    Carbs|**16g**

1 cup sugar
1 teaspoon ginger, freshly grated or 1/4 teaspoon ginger powder
1 teaspoon lemon juice, if using fresh fruits, for tossing

1/2 teaspoon salt (sea)
1/4 teaspoon cayenne pepper
1/4 teaspoon roasted cumin (ground)
2 tablespoons vinegar (apple cider)
4 cups (10 to 12 pieces) peaches, chopped

1. If using fresh fruits, wash them and dry. Remove the pits and chop into 1-inch chunks; peeled or skin-on. Mix with your lemon juice. If using frozen fruits, thaw to room temperature.
2. Put all of the ingredients in the IP. Mash the fruits using a hand blender or a potato masher to release some of the fruit juices. Lock the lid and close the pressure valve. Set to HIGH PRESSURE for 1 minute. NPR for 10 minutes when the timer beeps and QPR; unlock the lid and open.
3. Set the IP to SAUTE MORE mode; stir the peach mixture every 5 minutes or so till the texture is jam-like.  The fruit will splash as it boils towards the end of cooking so cover with a splatter screen if needed. Also, use a long-handled silicone spatula or wooden spoon to prevent splashes on your hands while stirring. Turn the IP off when the chutney is thick. Let cool before transferring to glass jars. Keep refrigerated for a couple of weeks or freeze for up to 3 months.

## Horchata or Sweet Mexican Rice Drink

Servings|**8**    Prep. Time|**5 minutes**    Cook Time|**11 minutes**
**Nut. Content (per 1 cup):** Cal|**133.8**    Fat|**2.6g**    Protein|**3g**    Carbs|**24.6g**

1/2 (14 ounces or 415 milliliters) condensed milk (sweetened, canned)
1/4 cup (65milliliters) rice (short-grain)
1/4 stick or 1/4 teaspoon cinnamon (ground))

1/4 teaspoon vanilla extract
2 cups (500milliliters) water
4 cups (1 liter) cold water

1. Mix 2 cups water, cinnamon, and rice in the IP. Lock the lid and close the pressure valve. Set to HIGH PRESSURE for 1 minute. NPR for 10 minutes when the timer beeps and QPR; unlock the lid and open. Transfer the mixture to a blender. Add the vanilla and milk; blend till the mixture turns to a paste.
2. Pour the cold water in a container (large). Add the pureed rice through a strainer (fine-mesh) into the water. Mix well and refrigerate to chill till serving time or serve over ice.

# FISH & SEAFOOD

## Thai-Inspired Seafood Curry

Servings|**4-6**    Prep. Time|**10 minutes**    Cook Time|**16 minutes**
**Nut. Content (per 6 servings):** Cal|**282**    Fat|**16.4g**    Protein|**16g**    Carbs|**19g**

1 tablespoon oil, coconut oil, peanut oil, or preferred neutral oil
1 tablespoon wet Thai curry paste (yellow, red, or green), or Penang curry paste.
1/2 cup coconut milk (low-fat or regular)
1/8 cup ginger (fresh), peeled & minced
3/4 cup onion and garlic, chopped

3/4 tablespoon fish sauce
3/4 tablespoon light sugar (brown)
3/4 tablespoon lime juice (fresh)
7 ounces (canned) diced tomatoes
2 to 5 chilies, hot green or red, for a spicier dish, optional

3/4 pounds shellfish or fish options:
Halibut fillets (skinless), chunked to 1-inch cubes
Medium shrimp (30-count per pound), peeled & deveined

Sea scallops
Swordfish (skinless), monkfish, cod, or hake (skinless) fillets, chunked to 2-inch cubes

1/2 pound veggie options:
Bell peppers, stemmed & seeded
Broccoli florets
Cauliflower florets
Chinese water spinach,
Green wax or preferred long beans, trimmed

Napa cabbage, cored
Squash (yellow summer)
Sugar snap peas
Zucchini

1. Set the IP to SAUTE for 10 minutes. Add the oil; let warm for 1 to 2 minutes. Add the onion and garlic; saute for 2 to 4 minutes or till soft. Add the ginger; cook for a couple of seconds. Add the curry paste; stir to mix well. Add the tomatoes, lime juice, coconut milk, fish sauce, and sugar; stir till the sugar dissolves. Press CANCEL.
2. Lock the lid and close the pressure valve. Set to HIGH PRESSURE for 7 minutes. QPR when the timer beeps; unlock the lid and open. Set to SAUTÉ for 5 minutes.
3. Let the sauce come to a full simmer. Stir in your preferred fish, shellfish, and veggies. Cook for 3 to 5 minutes or till the fish/shellfish is cooked through. Press CANCEL. Remove the inner pot from the housing. Serve warm.

# Tilapia Coconut Curry

Servings|**4**    Prep. Time|**10 minutes**    Cook Time|**10 minutes**
**Nut. Content (per serving):** Cal|**333**    Fat|**24g**    Protein|**25g**    Carbs|**6g**

1 pound tilapia fillets, sliced into 2-inch chunks, or tofu (extra-firm)
1 tablespoon garlic & ginger paste: 3 cloves garlic & 1/2-inch ginger, crushed or ground
1 tablespoon olive oil
1 teaspoon cumin powder
1 teaspoon garam masala
1 teaspoon salt
1/2 green pepper sliced
1/2 onion (medium), sliced
1/2 orange or yellow pepper, sliced

1/2 teaspoon chili powder (red) adjust to preference
1/2 teaspoon lime juice, to serve
1/2 teaspoon mustard seeds
1/2 teaspoon turmeric powder
10 curry leaves or 2 to 3 kaffir lime leaves
12 ounces (canned) coconut milk
2 teaspoons coriander powder
3 sprigs of cilantro
8 mint leaves: optional

1. Set the IP to SAUTE. After 30 seconds, add the oil and mustard seeds. When the seeds start to sizzle, add the garlic & ginger paste and curry leaves; saute for 30 seconds. Add the bell peppers and onions; saute for 30 seconds.
2. Add all of the spices; stir to mix well. Saute for 30 seconds. Add the coconut milk; stir to mix well. Let come to a simmer. Add the fish, a couple sprigs cilantro, and stir well to coat the tilapia. If desired, add a couple of mint leaves on top.
3. Lock the lid and close the pressure valve. Set to HIGH PRESSURE for 2 to 3 minutes. QPR when the timer beeps; unlock the lid and open.  Squeeze with lime juice. Serve with or brown rice, or slices of toasted baguette.

## Thai Tofu, Seafood, or Chicken Curry

Servings|6    Prep. Time|**10 minutes**    Cook Time|**10 minutes**
**Nut. Content (per serving):** Cal|**153**    Fat|**17g**    Protein|**17g**    Carbs|**14g**

1 cup (2 medium) carrots, chopped
1 cup baby corn, sliced
1 pound chicken thighs (boneless & skinless) or tofu (firm), cubed to 1-inch chunks
1/2 can curry paste (Maesri Thai Panang), or use the whole can
1/4 cup water
14 ounces (canned) coconut milk

After cooking:
1 cup florets broccoli
1 teaspoon sugar (brown)
Basil leaves (Thai), to garnish optional
A drizzle of lime juice

1. Prepare all the ingredients. Set the IP to SAUTE. Add the water and the coconut milk. Add the curry paste; whisk till well mixed. Add the carrots, baby corn, or your preferred veggies. Add the tofu, chicken, or seafood mix; stir to mix well. Let the mixture come to a simmer.
2. Lock the lid and close the pressure valve. Set to HIGH PRESSURE for 3 minutes. NPR for 5 minutes when the timer beeps and QPR; unlock the lid and open.
3. Adjust the seasoning as needed. Add the lime juice and sugar. Add the broccoli; let sit for 30 seconds to cook the florets with the residual heat for crunchy pieces. If you want them softer, SAUTE for 1 to 2 minutes. Serve with brown or white Jasmine rice.

## Fish Filets

Servings|40    Prep. Time|**5 minutes**    Cook Time|**12 minutes**
**Nut. Content (per serving):** Cal|**296**    Fat|**15g**    Protein|**23g**    Carbs|**21g**

1 bunch thyme (fresh)
1 clove of garlic, pressed
1 cup black olives, salt-cured, such as French, Taggiesche, Or Kalamata
1 pound (500 grams) cherry tomatoes, halved

2 tablespoons pickled capers
4 cod fillets or preferred white fish
Olive oil
Salt & pepper to taste

1. Put the IP steamer basket in the inner pot and pour 1 1/2 cups water. Line the bottom of a heat-safe bowl with the tomatoes and add the thyme; reserve a couple of the herb to garnish. Place the fish on top. Scatter the rest of the tomatoes, garlic, drizzle with the olive oil, and season with a pinch of salt. Put the dish on the basket.
2. Set the IP to HIGH PRESSURE for 4 to 5 minutes or to LOW PRESSURE for 7 to 8 minutes. QPR when the timer beeps; unlock the lid and open. Plate the fish in an individual serving platter. Top with the tomatoes, capers, olives, pepper, and drizzle with fresh olive oil. Serve.

## New England Clam Chowder

Servings | **4**    Prep. Time | **5 minutes**    Cook Time | **15 minutes**
**Nut. Content (per serving):** Cal | **320**    Fat | **14g**    Protein | **15g**    Carbs | **30g**

1 bay laurel leaf
1 cup (250milliliters) cream
1 cup (250milliliters) milk
1 cup bacon (cured & smoked) or pancetta, cubed
1 onion (medium), chopped finely
Pinch cayenne pepper (or flakes red pepper)
1 sprig thyme
1 tablespoon butter

1 tablespoon flour
1 teaspoon salt
1/2 cup (125 milliliters) wine (tarty white)
1/4 teaspoon pepper
12 to 24 clams (fresh), prepared, or 11 ounces or 300 grams strained canned or frozen clams
2 cups clam juice
2 potatoes (medium), skin-on, cubed

1. Put the bacon in the IP. Set the IP to SAUTE LESS mode. When the bacon starts to sizzle and the fat renders, add the onion, pepper, and salt. Set the pot to SAUTE NORMAL mode. Once the onion is soft, add the wine; scrape the brown bits off the pot. Let cook till the wine is almost completely gone. Add the potatoes and clam juice, adding enough water if you do not have enough for 2 cups. Add the cayenne pepper, thyme, and bay leaf.
2. Lock the lid and close the pressure valve. Set to HIGH PRESSURE for 5 minutes. QPR when the timer beeps; unlock the lid and open.
3. While the potatoes are pressure cooking, blend equal amounts of flour and butter in a small saucepan set over low heat, constantly stirring the mixture till well mixed.
4. Once pressure cooking is done, add the milk, cream, clam meat, and the roux; stir to mix well. Set the IP to SAUTE LESS mode; let come to a simmer. Cook for 5 minutes or till thick. Serve inside bread bowl or topped with soup crackers.

# Coconut Fish Curry

Servings|**0**    Prep. Time|**5 minutes**    Cook Time|**15 minutes**
**Nut. Content (per serving):** Cal|**248**    Fat|**14g**    Protein|**024g**    Carbs|**6g**

1 tablespoon ginger (freshly grated) or 1/8 teaspoon ginger powder
1 to 1 1/2 pounds (500 to 750 grams) fish fillets or steaks (fresh), rinsed & chunked into bite-size cubes, thaw if frozen
6 curry, kaffir lime, bay laurel, or basil leaves
1 tomato, chopped or 1 heaping cup cherry tomatoes

2 cups (500 milliliters) coconut milk (unsweetened)
2 garlic cloves, squeezed
2 green chilies, sliced into strips
2 onions (medium), sliced into strips
2 teaspoons salt adjust to preference
Juice of 1/2 lemon or ice to taste

Spices (or 3 tablespoons curry powder mix instead of the following):
1 tablespoon coriander (ground)
1 teaspoon chili powder or 1 teaspoon flakes hot pepper

1/2 teaspoon fenugreek or methi (ground)
1/2 teaspoon turmeric (ground)
2 teaspoon cumin (ground)

1. Set the IP to SAUTE. Once HOT, add the oil and curry leaves; fry them for 1 minute or till the edges are golden. Add the ginger, garlic, and onion; saute till the onion is soft. Add all of the spices; saute for about 2 minutes or till fragrant.
2. Add the coconut milk; scrape the browned bits off the pot and mix. Add the tomatoes, green chilies, and fish; stir to coat and mix. Lock the lid and close the pressure valve. Set to LOW PRESSURE for 5 minutes or to HIGH PRESSURE for 3 minutes. QPR when the timer beeps; unlock the lid and open.
3. Season with salt to taste. Drizzle with lemon juice just before serving. Serve alone or with cooked rice.

# VEGETARIAN

## Cottage Cheese & Spinach Gravy

Servings|6    Prep. Time|**10 minutes**    Cook Time|**015 minutes**
**Nut. Content (per serving):** Cal|**198**    Fat|**15g**    Protein|**8g**    Carbs|**6g**

1 green chili
1 onion (small), sliced
1 tablespoon garlic & ginger paste, 3 cloves
garlic & 1/2-inch ginger
1 tablespoon ghee or olive oil
1 teaspoon butter, optional
1 teaspoon cumin powder
1 teaspoon cumin seeds
1 teaspoon garam masala

1 teaspoon salt
1/2 teaspoon chili powder (Kashmiri red)
1/2 teaspoon turmeric powder
10 ounces block paneer (Indian cottage
cheese), chunked to 1/2-inch cubes
10 to 12 ounces baby spinach (bagged)
2 medium tomatoes chopped (about 1 cup),
OR 2 tablespoon tomato paste
2 teaspoon coriander powder

1. Set the IP to SAUTE. After 30 seconds, add the oil and cumin seeds. Once sizzling, add the garlic & ginger paste; sauté for 30 seconds. Add the green chili and onion; saute for 1 minute. Add the tomatoes; saute for 30 seconds. Add the spices and salt; stir well. Add 1/4 to 1/2 cup water; stir well. Lock the lid and close the pressure valve. Set to HIGH PRESSURE for 2 minutes. QPR when the timer beeps; unlock the lid and open.
2. Add the spinach. Set the IP to SAUTE; stir for 3 to 4 minutes or till the spinach is wilted. Turn OFF the IP. Puree the ingredients using an immersion blender.
3. Set the IP to SAUTE. Add the cheese; stir for 30 to 60 seconds or till the cheese is soft. Turn OFF the IP. Stir in the butter if using. Serve hot with naan or rice.

# Creamy Cottage Cheese

Servings|4    Prep. Time|**10 minutes**    Cook Time|**20 minutes**
**Nut. Content (per serving):** Cal|**398**    Fat|**35g**    Protein|**12g**    Carbs|**9g**

1 tablespoon garlic & ginger paste, 3 cloves garlic & 1/2-inch ginger, crushed
1 tablespoons cilantro, chopped (to garnish)
1 teaspoon cumin powder
1 teaspoon salt
1 teaspoon turmeric powder
1/2 cup cream (heavy)
1/2 onion (medium), chopped
1/2 teaspoon cardamom powder optional
1/2 teaspoon chili powder (red)
1/2 teaspoon paprika

1/2 to 3/4 cup water, or as the IP needs
10 ounces paneer (Indian cottage cheese), chunks into 1/2-inch cubes or tofu
2 tablespoons butter (unsalted)
2 teaspoon coriander powder
2 teaspoon fenugreek leaves or Kasoori Methi (dried)
2 teaspoon garam masala
4 to 5 tomatoes (medium), pureed, 14 ounces (canned) crushed or diced tomatoes

1. Set the IP to SAUTE. After 30 seconds, add the butter and onion; sauté for 1 minute. Add the garlic & ginger paste; sauté for 30 seconds. Turn OFF the IP. Add the tomato puree, water, and all of the spices; stir to mix well and deglaze the pot.
2. Add the fenugreek and 1/2 of the cream (save the rest for later); stir to mix well. Lock the lid and close the pressure valve. Set to HIGH PRESSURE for 3 minutes. NPR for 5 minutes when the timer beeps and QPR; unlock the lid and open.
3. Puree the mixture till smooth using an immersion blender or a regular blender and pour back into your cooker. Set the IP to SAUTE. Add the cottage cheese and the rest of the cream; simmer for 1 to 2 minutes or till desired texture is achieved.

# Quinoa Veggie Patties

Servings|**15**    Prep. Time|**10 minutes**    Cook Time|**20 minutes**
**Nut. Content (per patty):** Cal|**108**    Fat|**6g**    Protein|**2g**    Carbs|**9g**

1 onion (small), chopped finely (around 3/4 cup)
1 tablespoon olive oil
1 teaspoon coriander powder
1 teaspoon cumin seeds
1/2 cup peas (frozen)
1/2 cup quinoa, rinsed in a sieve (fine mesh)
1/2 cup water
1/2 teaspoon chili powder (red)
2 green chilies, optional
2 potato (medium gold), chunked into 1/4-inch cubes (around 1 1/2 cups)
2 teaspoons ginger, chopped finely or grated, or 1/2 teaspoon ginger powder
3/4 teaspoon salt adjust to preference
3/4 teaspoon turmeric powder

For patties:
4 tablespoons cilantro, chopped
1/2 lime juiced
1/2 cup preferred cheese, shredded

Coating (optional):
1/2 cup flour (all-purpose), cornmeal, or panko breadcrumbs

Pan-frying:
2 to 4 tablespoons oil per batch

Spicy mayo (mix well):
1/4 cup mayonnaise
1/4 teaspoon black pepper, crushed
2 tablespoons Sriracha

1. Prepare the ingredients before starting. Set the IP to SAUTE. Once HOT, add the oil and cumin seeds. Once sizzling, add the onions, ginger, potatoes, and green chili; saute for 1 minute. Add all the dry spices, peas, quinoa, and water; stir to mix well.
2. Lock the lid and close the pressure valve. Set to HIGH PRESSURE for 2 minutes. NPR for 10 minutes when the timer beeps and QPR; unlock the lid and open. Fluff the quinoa using a fork. Add the cilantro and lime juice; stir to mix. Let sit for five (5) to ten (10) minutes to cool before using. You prepare this quinoa mixture 1 day ahead.
3. Mash all the potatoes with a fork. Add the cheese. Stir to mix well. Wet your hands. Scoop the mixture using an ice cream scoop and form it into a patty with your hands; lightly coat with your preferred coating, shaking the excess off.
4. Heat a skillet (nonstick) over medium-high flame/heat. Add 2 to 3 tablespoons olive oil. Add the patties without overcrowding the skillet. Cook for 2 minutes or till the underside is golden. Flip and cook for 2 minutes or till the new side is crisp. Add more oil as needed. Serve.

# Vegetable Puffs

Servings|**12**    Prep. Time|**10 minutes**    Cook Time|**20 minutes**
**Nut. Content (per 1 puff):** Cal|**357**    Fat|**25g**    Protein|**7g**    Carbs|**25g**

Pastry shells:
12 Puff (1 pack, around 6 shells) Pastry Shells, thawed in the fridge

Filling:
1 gold potato, cubed into 1/2-inch chunks
1 tablespoon ghee or olive oil
1 teaspoon salt adjust to preference
1/2 inch ginger, finely grated, or 1/2 teaspoon Ginger Powder
1/2 teaspoon cumin seeds
1/2 teaspoon turmeric powder
1/4 cup bell pepper, chopped
1/4 cup corn (frozen), thawed for a couple minutes

1/4 cup peas (frozen), thawed for a couple minutes
1/4 to 1/2 teaspoon cayenne adjust to preference
10 ounces paneer (Indian cottage cheese), cubed into 1/2-inch chunks
2 tablespoons tomato ketchup
2 teaspoons coriander powder

After cooking:
1/2 teaspoon chaat masala
1/2 teaspoon roasted cumin (ground)

2 to 3 tablespoons cilantro, chopped

1. Line a tin pan using parchment paper or foil. Put the shells in the pan, placing them 1-inch apart. Bake following package instructions in a preheated oven. Let sit for five (5) to ten (10) minutes to cool before using.
2. Filling: Set the IP to SAUTE. Add the oil/ghee. Once heated, add the cumin seeds. Once sizzling, add the ginger and potatoes; stir to mix. Cover the pot with the IP glass lid or similar; cook for 2 to 3 minutes. Remove the glass lid. Add the paneer, tomato ketchup, spices, and veggies; stir to mix well. Cancel SAUTE.
3. Lock the lid and close the pressure valve. Set to HIGH PRESSURE for 0 minutes. QPR when the timer beeps; unlock the lid and open.  If the mixture is runny, set the IP to SAUTE; cook excess liquid for a couple of minutes till dry. Adjust seasoning as needed. Add the chaat masala, roasted cumin, and cilantro.
4. With your fingers or a paring knife, gently remove the center cap of the puffs; save the tops to cover the puff after filling if desired. Fill each puff with a couple tablespoons of filling. Serve with cilantro chutney, sriracha, or tomato ketchup. Save as snacks or lunch for kids.

# Yogurt Curry w/ Rice

Servings|**6**    Prep. Time|**10 minutes**    Cook Time|**20 minutes**
**Nut. Content (per serving):** Cal|**364**    Fat|**13g**    Protein|**12g**    Carbs|**48g**

Curry:
1 shallot (medium), thinly sliced, optional
1 tablespoon oil or ghee
1 teaspoon mustard seeds
1 to 1 1/2 teaspoon salt
1 to 2 green chilies (whole), optional
1/2 cup chickpea flour
1/2 teaspoon cayenne, adjust to preference
1/2 teaspoon fenugreek seeds
2 cups buttermilk or 1 1/2 cups yogurt
(plain sour)
3/4 teaspoon turmeric powder
4 cups water, use 5 cups if using very thick yogurt
6 to 7 curry leaves, optional

Rice:
1 cup PLUS 2 tablespoons water
1 cup rice (Basmati), rinsed 2 to 3 times
1 teaspoon oil
1/2 teaspoon salt

Onion-Spinach Fritters: skip for a simple curry
1 cup chickpea flour
1 teaspoon salt adjust to preference
1/2 teaspoon turmeric powder
1-2 teaspoon coriander
1 teaspoon chaat masala
1 teaspoon cumin powder, roasted
1/2 teaspoon cayenne adjust to preference
1/2 teaspoon baking soda
1/2 cup water adjust for pancake batter-like consistency
1 cup baby spinach chopped
1 shallot (medium) sliced thin or chopped
2 tablespoons olive oil (light) for pan-frying

Garnish:
1 teaspoon cumin powder, roasted
2 tablespoons cilantro, chopped

1. Curry: Sift the chickpea flour into the bowl with the buttermilk/yogurt. Add the water, cayenne, turmeric, and salt. With a wire whisk or a hand blender, mix till the batter is smooth.
2. Set the IP to SAUTE. Add the ghee. Once melted, add the fenugreek and mustard seeds. Once they begin to splutter, add the shallots/onion and curry leaves; saute for 1 minute. Add the buttermilk/yogurt; stir to mix well. Add the green chilies.
3. Set a trivet on top of the curry. Put the rice, oil, water, and salt in a small bowl and place on the trivet. Lock the lid and close the pressure valve.  Set to HIGH PRESSURE for 6 minutes.
4. While the curry and rice are cooking, make the fritters if using. Mix the chickpea flour, baking soda, and the spices in a mixing bowl (large). Mix with some water to reach pancake batter texture. Add the spinach and shallots; mix well.
5.  Heat pancake pan over medium heat. Add around 1/2 teaspoon olive oil in each cavity. With a spoon, scoop around 1 tablespoon of batter in each cavity. Cover with the lid; cook for 2 to 3 minutes, add more oil, flip, and cook for 2 to 3 minutes more. Alternatively, you can deep fry the fritters.

6. NPR for 10 minutes when the timer beeps and QPR; unlock the lid and open. Remove the bowl and the trivet. Set the IP to SAUTÉ. Add the roasted cumin; stir to mix. Add the fritters; simmer for 2 to 3 minutes or till they are soaked with the curry and soft. Serve warm garnished with cilantro over rice.

# Butter Cottage Cheese

Servings | **4**    Prep. Time | **5 minutes**    Cook Time | **15 minutes**
**Nut. Content (per serving):** Cal | **372**    Fat | **32g**    Protein | **11g**    Carbs | **9g**

1 tablespoon butter (unsalted) or olive oil (light)
1 tablespoon coriander powder
1 teaspoon salt
1/2 teaspoon turmeric powder
1/4 to 1/2 teaspoon chili powder (red)
10 ounces block paneer (Indian cottage cheese), chunked to 1-inch cubes
14 ounces (canned) diced tomatoes, or 3 to 4 tomatoes (ripe Roma), pureed
2 tablespoons garlic & ginger paste (1-inch ginger & 6 cloves garlic, grated or pulsed)

2 teaspoons paprika (smoked)
2 to 3 teaspoons garam masala adjust to preference

After cooking:
1 tablespoon fenugreek leaves (dried), optional
1/2 cup cream (heavy whipping) or coconut milk (full-fat)
2 teaspoons sugar
2 to 3 tablespoons cilantro (fresh), chopped

1. Set the IP to SAUTE. Once HOT, add the oil, ginger, tomato sauce, tomato paste, and spices; stir to mix well. Cancel SAUTE. Lock the lid and close the pressure valve. Set to HIGH PRESSURE for 4 minutes. QPR when the timer beeps; unlock the lid and open.
2. Add the paneer, fenugreek, cream, sugar, and cream/coconut milk. Set the IP to SAUTE, let come to a simmer. Cook for 3 to 4 minutes or till the cheese is soft and the sauce is thickened to preference. Serve garnished with cilantro.

# Spiced Cottage Cheese

Servings | **5**   Prep. Time | **5 minutes**   Cook Time | **10 minutes**
**Nut. Content (per serving):** Cal | **235**   Fat | **17g**   Protein | **10g**   Carbs | **10g**

1 green pepper, cubed
1 onion (medium), cubed
1 tablespoon coriander powder
1 tablespoon olive oil (light)
1 teaspoon cumin powder, roasted
1 teaspoon Indian five spice blend
1 teaspoon vinegar (red wine)
1 teaspoon garam masala
1 yellow pepper, cubed
1/2 teaspoon cayenne
1/2 teaspoon turmeric
1/2-inch ginger, finely grated

1/4 cup (around 1 medium) crushed tomato
1/4 cup water
10 ounces paneer (Indian cottage cheese), cubed
2 green chilies, cut a slit in the middle, leave whole
2 tablespoons cilantro, chopped, to garnish
2 tablespoons Yogurt (Greek)
2 tablespoons tomato paste
2 teaspoons fenugreek leaves
3 cloves garlic, chopped finely or grated
3/4 teaspoon salt

1. Set the IP to SAUTE. Once HOT, add the oil and five spice; let sizzle for 10 seconds. Add your ginger and your garlic; fry for around 30 seconds. Add the paneer, peppers, and onion; sauté for 1 minute. Add vinegar, spices, and salt; sauté for 1 to 2 minutes.
2. Mix the water, yogurt, crushed tomato, and tomato paste in a bowl (small). Add the mixture to a pot. Lock the lid and close the pressure valve. Set to HIGH PRESSURE for 0 (zero) minutes. QPR when the timer beeps; unlock the lid and open.

# Conclusion

In a world where most pressure cooker recipes are cooked for larger appliances, mostly 6-quarts, you can definitely use your 3-quart mini pot to its fullest potential in the kitchen, if you learn the valuable tips.

The MINI pot is as awesome as any larger cooker with its multi-cooker function and convenient features, and cooking recipes for its smaller size may does not always need testing in the kitchen.

Although it is not as easy as cutting down the ingredients for the recipes because of the various hidden modifications and variances can hugely affect how dishes are cooked for the mini models, you do not need to keep in mind the various variables or need to worry about the differences.

Numerous recipes are available that you can cook particularly for the Instant Pot Mini. No need to adjust any of the ingredients, measuring the liquids, or calculate about how much meat and veggies you can put in. You do not have to fear about overcooking or undercooking your dishes.

And if you if you already have favorite dishes that you make in a larger cooker, there are valuable techniques that you can use to successfully adapt them for your smaller MINI.

# Final Words

Thank you again for downloading this book!

I hope this book was able to help you start a wonderful adventure in the kitchen making delicious and healthy home-cooked IP MINI meals. I also hope you enjoyed reading and trying out all the wonderful dishes.

If you learned a great value about the IP MINI and loved the recipes, please leave a review. It will only take a minute of your time and I will greatly appreciate your thoughts!

Thank you in advance for your feedback! Happy IP MINI cooking!

Made in the USA
Lexington, KY
02 January 2019